Jesus
did
Not
start a
Religion

Robert Anthony

Sealed! Ministries
PO Box 1169
Auburn, WA 98071
JesusNotReligion.org

All Scripture quotations, unless otherwise indicated, are from the Holy Bible,
King James Version.

ISBN-13: 978-0-69267-942-5
ISBN-10: 0-69267-942-1

Printed in the United States of America

for my brothers…

Preface

The relational TriUnity of God's vision and mission, before the foundations of the world were laid and the creation spoken into existence was to reveal and manifest their holy character, divine glory, and the pure nature of their love. In the beginning, God's expression found form in the creation, the world, and the first Adam, made from the earth in the likeness of God's nature, with the Spirit of God breathed into man for the purpose of a CommUnity life with God.

God continued to reveal and articulate his nature in the people of Israel he called his own children, who manifested his glory, holiness and love—even if imperfectly. But they remain his beloved children.

In God's consummate expression, he manifested himself in his own Son. God is Spirit, yet has evidenced himself in flesh and blood, in his son Yeshua, born of a virgin by the Spirit of God in Beit-Lechem near Efrat, a small clan of Y'hudah (Micha 5:2) as 'Immanu El' (God is with us, Isaiah 7:14).

Why? Adam, the first man, became a living human being made in the image of God; but the consummate Adam, Yeshua the Son of God, has become a life-giving Spirit. He has pierced our time and space to live in CommUnity with us and to share his Spirit, which nourishes new life and a new creation, not to establish a religion.

The new creation and inauguration of his kingdom on earth (as is already known in heaven), ushers in peace and freedom—not a system of controlling power and binding ritual observances. Yeshua establishes a relationship in which we commune with God, not a system of devotion to doctrine. He transcends all our limited imagination and dwells in us as an overflowing fountain of life. He does not limit our access into the interiority of God's abiding love by requiring institutionalized observances under tyranny and fear.

What is to come in this book is a deeply personal account of a broken and contrite spirit who is redeemed, renamed, reshaped, and rejuvenated in the life-giving Spirit of our living God. May God be glorified!

Stephan E.
Switzerland

Foreword

When I first met Robert Anthony, he was "just" the speaker at a men's fellowship a new friend invited me to. But as I heard him sharing the stories of his life as a missionary around the world, I remember thinking, "This guy REALLY lives like the Bible talks about!"—and I was hooked! I wanted to "walk" with him, so I might learn to live so "biblically". I thought I was a "Bible-literalist", but I'd barely scratched the surface!

And how would ANY of us be anything else-especially if we grew up in church? Even in true Christian homes, as children we hear the stories of the Bible, then we read them for ourselves and we are just "naive" enough to think that those things should be part of OUR lives, TODAY! But as we grow, the "mature" Christians around us "explain" to us all their theological reasons why those things don't happen anymore-except on those RARE occasions when we, apparently, catch God in an uncharacteristic and inexplicably good mood and he deigns to drop a few crumbs from the table!

"Oh, slow of heart and unbelieving! How long must I bear with you?!?" I don't mean to pick on anyone, really, because most of those "mature" saints were-and still are-only passing on what got passed down to them! But what was REALLY going on when you believed those childhood stories was FAITH coming by hearing! And when you received-which most of us did-all that "theology" from those "mature" saints, you were receiving an impartation of UNBELIEF, plain and simple!

THAT was the world Jesus was born into, also! Even worse, actually! There was an entrenched religious system in place, with virtual power of life and death, that explained away EVERY good, happy, or pleasant thing about God. He was austere, impossible to please, and always angry! He certainly WASN'T a loving father whose family any of US would want to be born into! I've heard Robert say that the CHURCH, in actual practice, is supposed to "set" culture-instead of the other way around! The concept was so ALIEN to my mind, it took DAYS of reflection before I could accept it.

That is the kind of revolutionary (read that, "faith-filled") thinking you can expect from Robert. Jesus didn't "fit" into the religious system of his day. And he wasn't TRYING to be controversial. "Jesus went about doing good, and healing ALL who were oppressed of the devil." Could he help it if God wanted to do extraordinary and very PUBLIC miracles on the Sabbath? Jesus was only doing what he saw his Father doing. That's ALL he EVER did! And the words he spoke were ONLY EVER what he heard from his Father. Apparently, his Father wasn't very interested in catering to the religious system.

Let me say that another way; God is more interested in revealing himself to people and meeting their needs than he is about whether he steps on the toes of OUR religious customs and understandings. In fact, I'd say he doesn't alter HIS course AT ALL to avoid a collision. Like that battleship in the fog that kept honking at the approaching light, finally getting on their radio and angrily ordering them to change course. Back came the reply, "We are a lighthouse. Alter yours!"

What will WE do? We are either finding our identity in pleasing God or we are not! We are either flowing with the wind of the Holy Spirit or we are NOT! We are either living according to the Word of God or we are not. In his conversation with Nicodemus in John 3, Jesus likened EVERYONE born of the Spirit to the wind and said we don't know where it comes from or to where it's going. You're deceiving yourself if you think you can anticipate His next move. But the text ALSO says, ". . . where it comes from . . ." Don't think weathervane "technology" rendered Jesus' statement outdated.

We are either receiving men of God or we are not. We presume to "know" where men of God come from. But, do we, REALLY? Jesus answered and said to them, "Even if I testify about Myself, My testimony is true, for I know where I came from and where I am going; but you do not know where I come from or where I am going." John 8:14 NASB. I hope you recognize the parallel to John 3. How could they not know where Jesus came from?!? Surely, they had his genealogical records, so Jesus MUST have been referring to something else.

I tend to think it was his "ministry credentials," or apparent LACK thereof. We are so quick to judge those as "acceptable" who have made a name for themselves, or acquired many initials to follow their name or drawn large crowds of people or have lots of money. In John 8, Jesus said they were rejecting him because he was coming in his FATHER'S name, but if one came in his OWN name, they would have received him! Why do we think WE are different, today? God chose an old man and his barren wife to birth his chosen people. And what were Abraham's great-grandson Joseph's credentials? Slave? Prison steward? "Oh, let's recommend HIM to Pharaoh!" The story is the same throughout God's Word; He chooses the least and uses the unlikely, because His strength is demonstrated perfectly through our weakness. Only GOD'S way gives GOD the glory only HE deserves!

"Beauty is in the eye of the beholder", but we won't see the beauty of God's vessels if we don't value what God values. I've been blessed to spend many days with Robert since that first night I met him and he spoke timely words from the Lord to this one-time stranger. We've had many interesting and enlightening discussions about the Word of God. By the grace of God, I hope to have many more! But it's not his theology that won my heart. It was his simple, unassuming, humble approach to the Word of God and to life. He's childlike enough to be always listening for his Father's voice, so why should it be surprising that he so often hears it?

I've never knowingly or willingly ate locusts (although I've probably eaten wild honey), so I can't claim to have the credentials of John the Baptist. Nor am I related to Robert Anthony. Nevertheless, I am privileged to call him my friend, and truly, truly I say unto you, a truer friend I've NEVER had. I would commend this brother to you without ANY reservation or hesitation. So I also encourage you to take a deep breath and set aside all your assumed understandings of how Christianity "works", and just READ his book. Get a fresh taste of GRACE set loose in someone's life. It may even seem "Scandalous!" But maybe, just maybe, you'll get a fresh vision for what GOD could do through YOUR life—and the lives of others—and behold, HE would make ALL THINGS NEW!

Yours in Christ,
Phil B.
Seattle, Washington

Introduction

Jesus was a Jew. At no time in the life and ministry of Jesus do we hear Him saying anything like, "We are no longer Jews but now we are Christians." In fact for close to two hundred years the Christians were thought of as a sect of the Jews. The Bible tells us that in Christ we are "grafted" into that original "olive tree" who is Israel. So who are we as believers and followers of Christ?

I started to wrestle with these questions nearly two decades ago and I haven't stopped since. While some things have become clearer, I seem to have just as many questions as before. But it's okay. I have stopped living in those questions. Instead I have started to come to know God. Not just believe in Him but to actually know Him.

Lots of people believe in God but how many people actually get to know Him? How many people can say, honestly, transparent before the world, "I know God". In the same way I know friends and family I have come to know God. I have spent time with Him. I have listened to Him speak. I have been very privileged to have met the same God the men who wrote the Bible met. And He is still amazing and mysterious, yet I know Him.

I set out years ago to learn to live for Him. I mean truly with everything I have, live for God. It's been an amazing story let me tell you! I know I have so long yet to go but I really felt the Lord encouraging me to tell you all about my story and share what He has done with me these years. It's an exciting and adventurous story, full of ups and downs, trials and failures, breakthrough and triumph! There is plenty of suffering and joy, sorrow and pain but also the glory of God! It's been wild living it, let me tell you.

Sometimes when I tell my stories it all feels a little dreamy, even to me. I never would have imagined God giving me this kind of a life. Like I said, I feel extremely privileged and blessed! It's really the least I can do to share with you all what He has been doing with me these years. I believe that it will be an encouragement to your faith, an impartation of hope and a fire restored to your soul, beckoning you to love like never before!

It's easier to judge than it is to love. We can sit at home and judge, criticize and condemn without much effort or risk at all. But to live, to truly live this life with God, it's going to take a whole lot more than judgment and criticism. It's going to take heart! And not just any old heart. To truly live this life with God it's going to take all the love of God that can fit inside of us and even more than that!

We are going to get afraid. We are going to doubt. We are going to chose unbelief over trusting in our Father over and again. We are going to need new hearts if we are truly going to live this life with God! We will need God to take out our hearts of stone and give us New Hearts, hearts of flesh and blood, hearts that can break.

And Yes. If we have the courage enough to let God break us in such a way, if we will trust Him enough, He will put so much love inside of us that we will become *The Body of Christ* on the earth! If we will come to Him as children, He will take us away from our merely religious lives and He will lead us to Life! and *Life More Abundantly*! But it's going to take a lot of heart to follow Him there.

I believe some of you reading this testimony are ready and willing. I hope to inspire the rest. . . .

With love in Christ,
Robert Anthony

Chapter 1

I want to share with you the testimony of what the Lord has done with me all these years: I was seven years old when I received Jesus Christ into my heart. My aunt, my mother's older sister, had developed a terrible addiction to heroin, a very strong drug, and she was barely alive. It was a terrible time in our family.

My mother and her sister had a rough upbringing. They lived in fear because their father, my grandfather, was a criminal and a drunk. They had horrible lives living quite far from the presence of God. It's apparently a very natural thing for people who had hard childhoods like they did to start doing drugs.

I think perhaps my aunt just wanted to die, but in a last chance effort she went to a church service with a friend of hers from where she had worked part-time. The Holy Spirit was pouring out in that church in those days (soon thereafter the outpouring of the Holy Spirit ended, I have since learned). My Aunt Lori walked into that church in Las Vegas, Nevada, Sunday morning and God healed her miraculously and instantly! She was immediately set free of a very horrible, several year drug-addiction, without any withdraws or side effects! It was a genuine Jesus miracle, and everyone around Lori and the church knew it!

After much hesitation my mother allowed Aunt Lori to take my younger brother, Brian and I to that Holy Spirit-Alive Church. I received Jesus into my heart immediately. Shortly thereafter I was baptized and I became a totally new little person. I can still remember being baptized in a large swimming pool all these decades later.

My mom likes to tell stories about me becoming a seven-year-old little evangelist and telling people about Jesus wherever we went. She has stories of me preaching Jesus in a bank, in a grocery store and door to door, these are the stories that I can remember. God did something to this little boy! It was very clear to my mom. I was changed.

At that time my mother was learning to be a witch. She went to a school where they taught people to read palms, tarot cards, fortunes and other such things of the occult. She was preparing to have a career as a psychic (what we know to be a witch). When Aunt Lori showed up with Jesus in her life, my mom wanted nothing to do with it, but Lori was persistent, and my mom, finally let us go to church with her. When she saw the enormous and remarkable change of what God had made in me and her sister, she started to take note. Finally, after catching the witches in many lies, and realizing that Aunt Lori had in fact been healed, my mother gave her life to Jesus and then our whole family was saved! Everything changed; and changed quickly. My mom started to date this Jewish man named, Roger. She was so committed to Jesus by then that she would only date Roger if he promised to go to church with her. Roger was saved right away also! He became a "Jew for Jesus", and was very outspoken. He loved the Lord right away and his new found faith began to flourish! He and my mother were married a short time later.

My mom left my biological father, Bob, in Detroit before I was two years old. When I was four she married a man for a short period of time and then they also divorced. I had really wanted a husband for my mom and a father for my younger brother and me. Within a short time after Jesus came into my heart, He gave me a dad. It was very easy to love Jesus from the start. It was obvious to this little boy; God was in fact Good!

Life took many turns right away. The church where we had all found Jesus suddenly collapsed. They grew in three short years from 200-300 members to over 10,000. The power of God was present in that place and many people were healed, delivered and saved. It was a very exciting time. But then those younger pastors (in their 30's) got caught stealing money from the church, and at least one of them was cheating on his wife. That 10,000-member church where the power of God was so evident, fell apart almost as quickly as it grew. That was sad and very hard on our family.

My mom and dad basically blamed Vegas for it and said, "We don't want to raise the kids here anymore, this place is wicked, let's move to L.A." And just like that, my whole life changed, and changed and changed again. But the way I remember it, I was happy. Roger was a good dad: he never treated us like we were step kids. He began the process of adopting us. Those first years with Roger, we were very happy. We had Jesus! We were blessed!

Δ   Ω

I'm going to tell you as much of this story as I can without making it too long, but I'm still including the details I think are most important; there is much more I could write about.

Three of the first four churches we went to after I was saved, fell apart. The first, in Vegas, fell apart because of the pastors stealing money, and also from sexual immorality. The second church we attended is a very historically famous church, The Church on the Way, Jack Hayford was pastor; that church did not fall apart but its denomination grew and grew. The third church we went to in the suburbs of L.A. failed later due to the pastor cheating on his wife, with his best friend, an elder's wife. The fourth church we attended loved to preach about money, and how God will make you rich. It's ironic, but that church went under for not having funds enough to pay its bills.

Growing up was very difficult for me. I was twelve years old when I was baptized in the Holy Ghost, and the power of God was given to me. I noticed some very real changes in my life, especially the dissatisfaction of being in the world. Immediately, I became very sensitive to sinful things and I got rid of all my music collection because it wasn't Godly. After I received the Holy Spirit I had this great desire to please God, and again the desire to share His gospel as I had when I was just a boy.

Having this kind of a "fire" and sensitivity in you at a young age, in a very large, Los Angeles County school, is very difficult, to say the least. I knew many kids in junior high school who were already sleeping around and getting pregnant. It wasn't exactly a Godly or a holy environment at public school.

I remember once, getting kicked out of class because I wouldn't agree with the teacher that I had evolved from an ape. Quite sarcastically, I said, "Perhaps you evolved from an ape but I am sure I was created in the image of God." It really bothered me that I was so different. I wanted to fit it. But I couldn't. I tried. I started liking girls a lot in junior high school. Those years I was constantly being pulled by two very strong forces; the love of God and the spirit of the world.

My mom and dad argued a lot in those years; mostly about money (or our lack of it). They argued so much that I started to leave often when they would fight. I guess I was only ten years old when I started running away from home. When I was eleven I stole a pack of my father's cigarettes and forced myself to smoke. Then, for a short time thereafter, things got better. I was filled with the Holy Spirit but the hopelessness I felt in that public school and at home weighed too heavily on me. I made many other bad decisions in those years.

I was smart and gifted. I was placed in the highest level math class in junior high school, in seventh grade, but I lost interest in schooling rather quickly. I think it might have been all of the injustices that I kept facing; like being kicked out of classes for my firm rejection in evolution, etc. I wasn't a terrible kid; I was just gifted and hurt, filled with God's Holy Spirit and not understanding how to be a teenager (*in* the world but not *of* the world). It was a confusing and difficult time in my life, and high school got even worse.

I tried everything in High School to find somewhere I belonged: football, basketball, choir, Air Force ROTC, theatre and even partying. I tried to hang out with almost every click the high school had to offer, yet I felt at home with none of them. The only place I remember feeling at home in all those years, was my youth group. But we left that church when I was fourteen years old. Looking back, I don't even know how I survived and managed to graduate.

I moved out of my parent's house when I was sixteen years old. It's a miracle I survived that summer. I started drinking heavily and as I recall, probably got alcohol poisoning once or twice? I hit a rock bottom that summer, between my junior and senior year. My parents sent the cops after me at the end of the summer because I was not old enough to be living on my own. I came home a week or two before my senior year started, and right away I got mono (mononucleosis—what they call the kissing disease). I basically slept for two whole months until I got better.

It was a miracle that I graduated high school, but soon enough I was done. I was one small step away from being a grown up, but I had no idea what I would do with my life. In my heart Jesus was telling me that He had a plan for me, and that He was going to take care of everything. But I felt so hopeless it was nearly impossible to believe Him. Then a great miracle happened, and I knew that Jesus cared about me: *For sure!*

Δ   Ω

It was a week before the end-of-the-year senior party. Somehow I had been given the task of buying the alcohol for the party. I guess they all thought that I could talk my way into anything. The other seniors gave me something like $300 and I went to go talk someone into buying alcohol for us. I called up two of my friends with this 'great' idea, I said, "Why would we spend all this money when we could steal all the alcohol instead?" I guess I have always been a little adventurous, even misguided, but always ready for something exciting.

Our plan was simple; my friends would go into all the town grocery stores in the middle of the night, and grab all the alcohol they could carry and run out. I was to wait in the get-away car and speed off before anyone could grab us. We did this all night. We hit eight or so grocery stores late on a Wednesday evening and headed home.

It was summer in Southern California so it was hot in the evening. I was wearing shorts, a tank top and sandals. I was smoking something that looked like marijuana, but I never did those drugs, I was smoking an Indian cigarette. I wasn't speeding but still when a cop saw us on the way home and he decided to pull us over to see what we were up to. I will never forget this night.

He pulled us all out of the car and searched my Camaro. My heart dropped into my toes as I thought about going to jail, and how pissed off my parents would be. My trunk was completely full of stolen alcohol, maybe $500 worth!? Finally he finished his search and asked me to open the trunk for him. I can still remember praying to this day, "Lord if you get me out of this I will serve you. Please save me Jesus!" I put the key into the trunk to open it, very slowly . . . and suddenly the policeman's partner called out to him, "We have a (he used some three numbered code) we've got to go!" The cop looked at me, before I had a chance to open the trunk, and he said, "This is your lucky day kid. Go home. If I see you out again tonight I will arrest you."

My friends were still seated on the curbside and I fell to my knees as the cops pulled away. I couldn't help but weep. I should have gone to prison for what I had done, but instead the Lord had mercy on me. I totally deserved to go to jail, but God loved me and gave me a break. My life truly would have gone in a very different direction had I gone to jail then. It was a real Jesus miracle. I knew then for certain, without a doubt, that God loves me.

I graduated from high school a month after that evening, and moved to Seattle Washington for Bible College. I did as I said I would and I began to walk with God, with all my heart. Jesus had given me a fresh start and I was eager to learn to walk with Him. I really wanted to grow up to become a good man . . . a man of God. Hope filled me for the first time in many years and I became a new person.

God began teaching me how to walk with Him as a man. It was a very exciting time of life.

I was happy again . . . for the first time in many years.

Chapter 2

What really added to my hopelessness as I was growing up was the religion I was around. There was some *Spirit-of-God* but there was also a *lot of religion*. I will explain as I tell you the story.

Every Sunday morning when we would be getting ready for church it seemed my mom and dad would get into a terrible fight. By then my brother and I had two little sisters, who would be crying, and Brian and I would usually get angry. Finally, we'd arrive at the church and be forced to pretend we were happy, as though the chaos back at home never happened.

There were so many things that confused me about 'church'. I was hurting as a kid. I wanted to stop hurting, but it seemed like no one knew what to do with me. I tried to talk to people about it, especially my youth pastor, but nothing really seemed to work. Looking back, I was angry. I was hurt and angry, but I didn't know why. I knew that something was wrong with me, but I couldn't say what it was? I seemed to get some comfort at church, but not much was changing in me. The Youth Group gave me more hope, but that was short lived.

Finally, I got to Bible College. I was a young man and I began to find my own way. Soon I came to the conclusion that Jesus was in fact able to help me. I did everything I could to learn from the men of God around me. I had many mentors and elders those years, and many of them gave me wonderful gifts and wisdom. But none of them came close to being a substitute for my time with Jesus.

I began to learn how to pray and hear His voice, not so much in class but more so during my time with friends at *home meetings* and such. I had a pretty large group of friends who all seemed to want to know God better; and walk with Him every day. It was usually outside of class that I had my best and most life altering times in the presence of God. Whether we were singing and praising Jesus at home (I lived with Fred then in a one-bedroom house with five other guys) or we were at a bible study somewhere else, it was those times with friends, gathered in Jesus' name that made the biggest and longest lasting impression. I had to literally forget much of what I learned in Bible classes because it was wrong, not all of it, but a lot of it. Many well intentioned people instilled much of the religion within me.

I learned to really enjoy hard work while in Bible College. I took on many jobs in order to afford living on my own, and along the way I gained a genuine enthusiasm for working hard. I was eighteen years old and quickly becoming a man. I was also becoming a man of God, but not as quickly. Gifts that God had put inside of me were beginning to come out. I came to believe that, in fact, God had a purpose for me.

Δ   Ω

I had come home to L.A. for a Christmas break with Craig, a dear friend of mine. When I got home I couldn't stop thinking about Erik, a friend that I had known since elementary school. I had to find him. I didn't know why, but I knew I had to find him. It had been many years since I had lost communication with him. We had grown apart in high school because he started doing drugs and stopped going to school. Something was compelling me to find Erik, but I did not yet realize that it was God.

Finally, one afternoon Craig and I went to the last place I remember Erik living, and knocked on the door. A very grungy and depressed looking Erik answered with a look of disgust and unbelief on his face. He said "What the **** are you doing here?" I was surprised by his greeting, but I could tell he was going through a very hard time so I didn't let it bother me. He left the door open and walked back inside. We followed him in.

I saw bottles of pills that had been emptied on his coffee table. He was preparing to commit suicide that day. He showed me the note he had just written as he wept. He asked me, "What are you doing here?" He couldn't believe that I had just randomly showed up after all these years, just moments before he was about to take all those pills!

We wept together as we felt God's love for him. Of course we knew it was a miracle. God had saved his life! Trying to calculate the odds of me showing up when I did after not seeing him for so long, could only have been a miracle. Erik realized that day, without a doubt that God loves him. He decided not to kill himself. Years later Erik became a banker and married a beautiful girl. Last I heard they were blessed and very happy.

Another time during Bible College years, a few friends and I decided to start going door to door and praying for people. We would get together on Saturdays and simply knock on doors and ask if we could pray for them. Usually the answer was "No" but there were a few times that miracles happened.

This one time I went up to a door and God told me to tell this man, "You don't have to worry about money. God knows your need and He is going to take care of you." The house wasn't in bad shape or anything, but I decided to trust God anyway and tell the man. As soon as he answered the door he slammed it in my face saying, "I don't want any." I have been told a time or two that I can be bold, so I knocked again. This very tall, lumberjack looking man opened the door, this time all the way and said, quite angrily, "I told you. I don't want anything from you!" I responded, "Well look, the Lord told me as I walked up here to tell you not to worry about money anymore. That He is going to take care of everything..."

The man looked at me with shock and awe. He said, "What did you say?" I repeated what the Lord told me to say. I watched in amazement as this massive and intimidating beast of a man started to weep and said to me, "Yes. Please pray. God sent you here. My wife is in the hospital dying of cancer and I was just sitting down trying to figure out what I can do to pay all the bills. They want to kick her out because I don't have any more money." He wept as I prayed for him. While I don't know what happened with that man I'm sure God took care of him, just like He promised.

One day, during praise and worship at church, a man kept trying to raise his hands. But every time he tried it was as if someone had punched him in the stomach and he would keel over in pain. The song continued and he lifted his hands again, only to receive the same invisible blow to the torso. The Lord told me, "This man has a demon and he needs to be delivered". I felt compassion for him and I tapped him on the shoulder and asked if I could pray for him?

The man looked at me with a certain pitiful desperation and said, "Please." I motioned for him to follow me over to the side of the aisle, out of the way, trying not to make a scene. I had never cast a demon out of anyone before, but I had read the bible a lot, so I did what Jesus did in the Bible; I said, "In Jesus name, I command you demon to come out of the man!" I began to put my hand on his chest but before I could, he shot back six to eight feet and started writhing around on the ground like a snake or a worm. It was incredible to watch!

Minutes later, he got up off the floor and he looked like a totally different person. That pitiful look of despair was totally gone and his face was full of light. He ran to the front of the church and began to Praise God, hands lifted high. It was incredible to be a part of that moment. But then I was horrified as I watched the security people run over to him and pull him away from the altar in the front of the church. He had just been set free of perhaps years of demonic possession/oppression, but no one was interested in hearing his story or even wanting to know why he was upfront, praising God with such joy. I was troubled to say the least, seeing how he was being treated. It grieved the Spirit of God that the whole church didn't know what Jesus had just done for this man.

Δ Ω

Bible College years did not get much easier on the heart. The brokenness of the religion was right in front of me, plain to see, on a regular, almost daily, basis.

I was put on some kind of leadership counsel for the school; giving me access to much of the schools behind the scenes personal information. One day we were reviewing a fax from a very well-known TBN preacher who was going to come and preach at our Bible College. On the fax was a list of demands that would be required for him to come and preach for one afternoon. The first line item (and I will never forget it) was, 'A Minimum $10,000 Honorarium'; that was a long time ago when $10,000 was a lot of money. But that list of demands just got worse and worse. He required a white limousine to pick him up from the airport, a weekend stay at the Four Seasons in downtown Seattle, and many other very offensive line items.

The list went on and on ... he was a pastor who would have been preaching at our Bible College, he wasn't a rock star performing at our venue. I was offended and grieved to say the least.

Another time during Bible College, I was at a huge pastor's conference just outside of Seattle and the main speaker commanded the pastors in the room, saying, "You pastors need to learn to run your churches more like a business!" And it seemed everyone in the room shot to their feet in applause, even shouting in agreement. I was appalled! Did my Jesus die so that we could become big institutional leaders, captains of religious industry and high-paid, motivational speakers? I was shocked, offended and angry.

I could continue to tell stories of all that I saw those years, the good, the bad and the really bad, but I have painted a pretty good picture of what Bible College was like for me. God began to show me the problem. He opened my eyes, slowly at first. I was already sharing in God's burden for His precious flock. I didn't know why He chose me for this.

The first real sermon I ever preached was at Bible College (I remember preaching in youth group but I don't remember much about it). It was for the biggest part of my grade in a preaching class. I had written a very good sermon I thought, but the night before I was to preach, the Lord told me He had something else for me to say; and He told me not to prepare. That night the Lord revealed to me a truth, a simple but very powerful truth, "Jesus didn't do it the way we do it." I wrote those words on the white board and then I began to preach.

Throughout my sermon, I explained that we gather masses of people together days, weeks or months in advance, but Jesus lived each day unto itself. I talked about how we rule over the church, like kings with large staffs and budgets; but Jesus stripped Himself naked and like a servant and washed His Disciples feet. All throughout my sermon I kept repeating the line, "Jesus didn't do it like we do." It was very quiet while I was up there.

When my sermon was finished, how many people out of a classroom of 40 people do you think were applauding me? You guessed it. *Not one.* There was utter silence as I took my seat. I was nineteen years old, rather insecure, and intimidated by the caliber of men in that room. I was by far the junior man. I thought I had failed the Lord, miserably. And I couldn't wait to run out and away from the school, to sulk. As I sat in the classroom waiting for it to finish, no one would talk with me. I wanted to leave so badly.

Finally, the class was over and I left; head hung low. The dean of the college was in the class that day and listened to my sermon. He walked next to me down the hall and said, "Robert, do you want to know why I think no one clapped for your sermon?" I was surprised by his question. But I hoped to hear some better news than what I thought had happened so I nodded, "Yes". He said, "Robert, I am a 60+ year old man and I have heard hundreds if not thousands of sermons but I have never ever heard a sermon like that before. God has given you a special gift and a message for the Body of Christ. You have to know that. I believe that God is going to do something incredible with your life."

I felt better hearing his words, for sure. But I didn't totally agree with him. I thought maybe he was just being nice, but he did give me some new things to think about. Maybe God did have a great plan for my life? Maybe God was in fact going to do something amazing with me and through me? Oh how I hoped!

Δ   Ω

Things took a terrible turn as I was finishing up Bible College. I started dating this girl who would ultimately ruin me, for years to come. It's a long sad story. But I ended up losing my virginity to her and my hope was yet again stolen from me. I was very down on myself, and it took many years for me to forgive myself for what I had done with her and to her.

While I was dating her I was invited to preach at a church near the Bible College. To this day I am not sure why they sent me? But I was chosen. The message that the Lord gave me was again a little hard to hear. What I received from the Holy Spirit was, "Let's try to be less religious." I talked a lot about evangelism and how we use words that these people have never heard before. We start telling people about Jesus and we use words like: *grace, righteousness, salvation, born-again* and *redeemed*. But these unchurched people have little to no understanding of words like this.

I preached boldly about becoming lovers instead of bible bashers. I don't remember everything I said, but I do remember that when I was finished, again I got not *one* iota of applause. They didn't even smile at me when I was through. The way I remember it is that they ignored me completely and I was left alone with a friend of mine named Jakki, who did a very good job comforting me, assuring me what I said was good and that it needed to be said. Jakki has always been a good friend (I am sad to this day by what became of our friendship.)

It seems that throughout my late teens and twenties as I would see the brokenness of the world, I would become overwhelmed and hopeless. I believe this is why I hid out in sins so often throughout my early twenties. The feeling of hopelessness was more than I could bear and it often seemed easier to escape from these feelings into the false comforts of sin than it was to face them, with Jesus. I have since learned a better way.

I broke my first girlfriend's heart, for sure. I hope that she was able to forgive me. I hoped that many of those girls who would come after her would be able to forgive me. I have fallen far short of the example of what a man of God should look like. But still, He has given me so many very precious things to give the Body of Christ. I don't know why He chose me to have these precious things. Many times I have argued with Him and tried to get Him to change His mind, but He kept encouraging me onward. He never gave up on me. Perhaps I was doing everything I could to be faithful, even when I would fall? It's hard to judge.

Bible College ended with a lot of tears and heartache. The Lord made me into a young man of God in Seattle Washington, but I still had so very far to go. I was nineteen years old when I finished my two years of college. Then, again, God did a great miracle to lead me into business after I was done.

He has always had a plan for my life. It's been quite the adventure.

I will continue to tell you about it.

Chapter 3

I was working for the airlines in Seattle, so I could fly practically for free. Since flying was so cheap I usually flew first class (if seats were available). Just before graduation, while flying home to L.A. for a weekend get-a-way, I was praying about what God would do with me and writing down what I was hearing from Him in my journal. I have often kept prayer journals. It has been fun to watch God answer prayers over the years. (*Now I keep prayer and dream journals because of how often God communicates with me through dreams and visions*). Sitting on the flight next to me was an older, attractive, Asian woman in a business suit.

The Asian businesswoman was very curious about a young man like myself flying first class. She asked me, and I explained to her that I worked for the airlines and was able to fly very inexpensively, even first class. She asked me lots of questions. I don't know what made her so curious about me. She asked me questions about college and my life, and what I was hoping to do. Finally, I shared with her what I had been writing about in my journal.

I really felt that the Lord was putting me in business. Even though I had gone to a Bible College and had the schooling to become a pastor, I didn't feel that was the path that the Lord had me on. And then she started to encourage me to go into banking!? She ran a division of Washington Mutual Bank, and was a very senior person over their mortgage division. I had never even heard of the word *mortgage* before. She was so convinced that I should get into mortgages that she said, "If you don't get a job call me and I will make sure Washington Mutual in L.A. hires you."

When I got home to my parent's place in the suburbs of L.A.
I told them about all that had happened. They said, "This is the
Lord!" It turned out that a Jewish friend of my dad's was a mortgage broker and owned a rather large company near our home
town. My dad had been talking to him about me and they had
already planned, before I landed, a meeting with him and me. It
was another Jesus miracle!

Long long story short, I was hired to be the right hand intern
of the number one mortgage broker in town. He taught me
everything about the business and within a short while I was
a mortgage officer, writing my own loans with my own clients.
I was nineteen years old. My life was suddenly exciting; taking
off like a rocket.

I was so used to living with that sense of hopelessness and
fear that as things started to go so well for me, I really had to
go to God so that He would change some things in my heart. It
was strange but I had to learn how to be happy, I had to learn
to accept the good things from God. I was so used to suffering
and heartache that blessing and abundance was uncomfortable for me.

Δ Ω

There were a lot of ups and downs those first years in business.
It was very hard to learn so many new things, so fast. As a lender
you have to know about taxes, banking, other loans, insurance,
stocks and other investments. Mortgage lenders have to know
about the financial industry at large to be able to accurately
advise their clients about which loan is best for them. It was
a lot for a nineteen-year-old to learn (who had practically no
business education whatsoever. Remember, I graduated from
Bible College.) Those were challenging years but I have always
enjoyed a good challenge.

Even with all the ups and downs I took off in business like a
racehorse coming out of his stall. Within a short year and a half
I was partnered with another mortgage guy and I managed to
run a small office for him, 20 miles from my house. He ended up

stealing from me ($30,000) and trying to ruin me in business. I quickly realized I would have to do this by myself. By 22 years of age I started my first mortgage company. It was a very exciting and fast paced time of life. Still I managed to attend church services, read my bible and pray. But certainly my relationship with God was diminishing.

During those same years my parent's marriage went down the tubes. Roger, the Jew for Jesus, and my precious, yet strong-willed mother, had been arguing for years. They even separated at one point in time, but then they got back together, renewed their vows and had another wedding ceremony. But nothing they tried worked. They were divorced a year or so after they had renewed their vows. It was a very sad, horribly tragic and overwhelming time for a young guy trying to make his way in the world. Our whole family was hurting and it wouldn't end for quite some time.

Then the start of a very dark time of my life came. I wasn't finding a church where I fit in. All the churches I kept visiting in L.A. seemed to love money, or be comfortable living in sin, or were just plain religiously dead. It was like the perfect storm: no church family, my family fell apart, my friends were mostly worldly business people (or old friends from high school) and I was making a lot of money. The perfect storm for sure...

I couldn't find solace in the churches. I couldn't find comfort with any of my family . . . so I started drinking. Of course it was a bad decision, but that's what people do who feel overwhelmed with hopelessness. One day I prayed, "Lord, I can't go to these churches anymore. I just keep getting hurt there. Please don't leave me." I can still remember that prayer to this day. Slowly my spiritual life was replaced by partying (again) and I fell back into great darkness.

Truly, I didn't really enjoy being drunk. I hated the feeling that came the morning after the parties, often the people at these parties were not my friends at all, but with that hopelessness what else was I to do? Parties, girls, money, pot a few times, those years went by, not nearly fast enough. I needed to be saved again. I needed Jesus but I didn't know where to go to find Him.

Δ   Ω

It was 2002, I was at a party with many celebrities, and one drink away from being completely drunk. I will never forget that night. We went to the party in a limousine, and my very wealthy friend was trying to talk these two Swedish models into leaving with us. He said, "Don't worry. I can buy your love." I could have thrown up right there. Even with all the broken life I was living I still had Jesus in my heart. I still had the Holy Spirit pulling at me. I was never happy in those bars. I was miserable for several years.

Try to imagine knowing the presence of God and His goodness, having seen Him move mightily in your life in so many ways and yet falling into this pit. I was not happy. Even though I tried to fake it and be the life of the party, inside I was miserable. After I heard my friend saying all this ridiculousness to these girls, I left him. I went and hid myself, off to the side of the party, and prayed, "Jesus please save me. I can't do this anymore. I am miserable. But I don't know what to do? I don't know where to go."

It was amazing! I heard the Lord respond to me immediately! There in the midst of all that drinking, music and partying I heard the voice of God, He said, "I am with you." That made me weep. "Why are you here with me?" I asked. I couldn't believe what He had just said. I didn't understand why He would say such loving things to me even though I was doing so many bad things. He said, "I will never leave you. I will never forsake you." I just sat there trying to hide from all those people, looking out over the L.A. basin and I wept. Suddenly I knew that God was always with me. Suddenly I knew again, God loves me. He never left me even though I had done all these terrible and sinful things. My life changed that night. I met Jesus, all over again.

I started to pray and read the bible again. I still went to parties sometimes, but usually I ended up being the designated driver and I wouldn't drink at all. Joy was returning to my life. I was starting to hear the Lord again; I was returning to the practice of dwelling in His presence. Looking back it was amazing how quickly He returned me to Himself. I didn't even have to pay a penance or "work" myself back into His good graces.

One night not long after I had encountered God at the party, the Lord woke me. I had been praying diligently about what I would do with my life, being that I couldn't find a church that I felt safe in and I still didn't have a family. The Lord said, "Robert, I never started a religion." It was just that simple. He didn't expound on it, but the revelation that came to me as He spoke those words, was as if I was Neo in the Matrix and I was having something downloaded into my brain.

I reread the whole New Testament that weekend. It wasn't in there. God was right. He never started a religion. Of all the things Jesus did, He never built a building, He never created some name for Himself and His followers; He never organized them into some kind of hierarchy. Jesus did not start a religion! It was all right there in front of me, written down so clearly in the New Testament. How come I had never seen it before? Jesus truly didn't do it the way we do it.

I lost nearly all interest in partying overnight. I had to know more about what the Lord was showing me. Every morning I started the day by digging through His Word. I got rid of my television. Every night I searched the scriptures instead of watching movies. Often I would go to a coffee shop and study well into the evening. I had to understand this revelation. What was my God showing me?

Ironically, during this time I started to go back to visit some of the churches I hadn't set foot in a church in some two years; I just had to be with God. Even though they were broken and clearly not living in the love of God, I wanted so badly to praise God again. I wanted to be with the saints of God and gather and find brothers. I must have visited every church in L.A. during those years.

As God gave me more from His scriptures I began to share, slowly at first, the things He had shown me. Often I was rejected, but sometimes those men would agree with me. As time went by I realized that God had given something very special. I had to do something with all this revelation. But what?

Δ   Ω

Just after I started walking with God again I went back into therapy, or counseling. This man Richard was about to make a huge, life changing impact on the young man, Robert. What started with lots of friction and tears, ended up becoming a wonderful relationship! Richard was the sage and I was his pupil. One of his catch phrases, I will never forget, "I am here to help you to find a *territory beyond fear!*" He was/is this amazing gem hidden behind years of rejection and hurt. But the Lord gave him to me. I received everything I could from him. Richard was such a blessing!

Richard had made some waves years back as a pastor of a strict, religious denomination, and they treated him very harshly, so he was removed. In truth, he had done nothing Biblically wrong, but he disagreed with the organization and soon their leadership wanted him out. I really don't remember the whole story. But what I do remember is the hours of talks, as I shared my heart with him, and he helped me to find healing in Jesus' name. He helped me to discover that my heart was broken and led me on a path with Jesus to have it healed.

The biggest thing he helped me to see was that I really didn't know God very well at all. My view of God was totally skewed. I saw Him more as a Judge or Dictator than a loving Father. God used Richard to show me the scriptures all over again. The Spirit of God moved mightily in our meetings; I was being changed. I had come out of so much condemnation those years, but finally I was finding freedom. Freedom like I had never known before. God loves me! I was coming to understand much more about what that means.

Around the time I was hanging out with Richard, maybe three years after the divorce was over, my dad, Roger, called me and said, "I got in touch with Bob, your biological dad and he wants to meet you!" What was I to say? I was 23 years old and the only memory I had of Bob, my biological father, was him spanking my brother and I felt totally powerless against him. I must have been three years old in that memory. Why did Roger get in touch with Bob? It was a very strange thing for him to do, I thought. But God was doing so many things in my heart at that time that I decided maybe that God was in it. One day I called Bob and we started to talk.

Bob had also found Jesus! He told me a long story about how Jesus had come into his life and all the amazing things that God had done for him over the years, freeing him from alcohol, taking away lots of his anger, etc. The more we talked the more I wanted to meet him face to face.

Finally, I bought a plane ticket and flew out to Detroit, Michigan, my birthplace, to meet my long lost dad.

I was 23 and my life was about to change, again, forever.

Chapter 4

Flying out to meet my dad was a great adventure. The whole flight and waiting for him at the airport, I was totally in shock. Looking back maybe it was helpful that he was an hour late to pick me up but at the time I was not happy about it. I was perfectly prepared to be upset with him for making me, his long lost first born son, wait at the airport for an hour; but then he pulled up. My dad jumped out of his SUV so fast he practically forgot to put it into park. He ran over to me, grabbed me in his arms and said, "My God! My son! You are so beautiful!" He hugged me and kept saying over and again, "You are beautiful, Robert! Look at you!" And he continued to hug me. Now how could I be upset at someone like that?

It was strange how familiar it felt to be with him. Even after all those years; and really never knowing him. I was so comfortable being with my dad that I actually started to feel uncomfortable, as I tried to figure out why I was so comfortable with him. It was an overwhelming as we drove to lunch as I tried to stay in the moment with my dad. I was actually in Detroit, with my real dad, going to lunch.

On the way to eat he took me to the house where I was born. It had, in fact, been torn down, but he hadn't realized it. We were in a very bad part of the city of Detroit. He told me not to unlock the doors or look at anyone. Finally, he asked me, "So you must have some questions for me?" I said, without much hesitation, "Well, yeah, what happened to you all these years? And why did you never want to come and find us?" You could see his expression change quickly and the happiness fade away from his lips. I kinda felt bad after I asked him that question so directly, with such a tone.

But he seemed to be fine with my direct approach. He said, "Yeah. Of course you want to know that." As we got to the restaurant he began to tell me everything about his life, about his childhood with his difficult father, and about meeting my mother. He told me about when I was born and how my mother left him. It was a very sad story all in all. What was so shocking about my dad's story was how different my mother's was from his. It was almost night and day, so different. It was hard to not be upset with my mother having heard all that he was telling me, and realizing that I only heard her side of the story for all these years. (Not that I blame her. But that fact still remained: my dad had his own way of looking at things.)I can write chapters about meeting my dad. There are so many other stories I could be telling but I am trying to be brief.

Things went ok with my dad that first trip. It was very hard to be open with him. I felt like a rock the whole time I was in Detroit. Not only did I meet my dad but I also met my maternal grandfather, my mom's dad. I met my paternal grandmother, my dad's mom; I met aunts and an uncle, my dad's brother and sisters. I was on emotional overload to be sure. My mom's dad was so ashamed about the criminal life he had lived that when I brought it up he wouldn't even talk about it. He didn't want to glamorize any of that life. I actually appreciated that he did that for me. Made me feel like he was protecting me, like he was loving me. He passed away shortly after I met him. I wish I had known him better, he was surprisingly loving and caring.

Then on the flight home, as I got comfortable in my seat, this cute 30-something year old single girl who was sitting next to me, started to talk to me. She asked, "So what were you doing in Detroit?" It was strange, but tears started to stream down my face as I told her about meeting my dad for the first time. I wept like a child the entire five-hour flight home to L.A. She was an incredibly good friend to me, comforting me and keeping me talking. She was so good at listening. It was like she had been trained to help people talk about their hurts. I was crying so loudly, I probably made many people on that flight feel uncomfortable. But I couldn't help it. God was healing some places very deep inside of me.

I had thought of meeting my dad a time or two throughout my life but what I never imagined was that I would actually like him. Furthermore, it never even once occurred to me that I would love him. Truth be told, my dad was/is very easy to love. It is horribly tragic that we didn't get to know each other throughout our lives. God was in it to be sure. Bob was a very different person before he found Jesus. But I had never in my whole life considered that I would enjoy to being with my dad.

There were many ups and downs after that first trip, but all in all, it was a huge success. Brian also ended up going out to meet him, and we all tried to make a family out of the mess. There was so much against us, so many years of hurt to overcome. And now I was a full grown man with my own life in Los Angeles. But we tried as best we could to become father and son. There would be many years of suffering and trials to come as we struggled to make the best of it. It seemed as though most everyone was against us, his family, my family, no one was interested in letting us get close. Certainly there was *the* enemy against us every step of the way (Ephesians 6:12).

Δ Ω

As God was healing me from things in my childhood, and other hurts from not having my dad, He was also healing me from other fears, doubts and sins that I struggled with. Those years began a season of healing for me. That is not to say that I was completely healed back then, but my heart was definitely being healed in some very deep places by the Lord.

Things that used to be desirable just went away. I stopped drinking completely. I had been smoking on and off since I was ten or eleven but I stopped smoking completely. I even stopped dating . . . well for the most part . . . God was healing me, and it was showing up in aspects of my life. I was a slow work God was doing, but I was becoming a completely different person none the less.

I remember the book, "Wild at Heart" had just come out and it made a very big impact on my life then. Hannah Hunard's "Hinds feet in high places" was also a big influence on me. But mostly I was reading the Bible. I was filling journals, attending prayer meetings, being with the Lord and reading the bible for hours every day. I was so happy as Jesus made me healthy.

God had become my Father all over again. It was awesome! Saturday's I didn't even want to work or go hang out with friends. Often I would take my guitar and go to a park; just playing music, sing and write and spend the day being quiet before God. I remember, during those years, finding a Franciscan Retreat Center in Malibu, and going to learn to just sit and be still before God. My life was changing dramatically as I learned to abide in His presence. I was happy during those years (2003–2005).

My mom and Roger-dad continued to fight. It made me want to stay very far away from them. But I loved them both and wanted them to be happy. However, there was nothing I could do. For the most part I was staying away from my dad. He was getting more and more upset; he was hard to be around. The bitterness was taking him over. It was not fun to watch.

I hadn't seen my dad in six months, so one day I decided to drop in on him. He had moved in with his girlfriend (I think that they were engaged then?). I went there to surprise him. I knocked on the door but he was not home, his soon-to-be adopted daughters, told me that he would be back soon and that I should wait for him. Only moments later he pulled up with his girlfriend/fiancée.

He looked incredibly angry getting out of the car. And he motioned for me to meet him down in the street. I went down with him, wondering what he was doing? He began taking off all his watch and jewelry; asking me strange questions. He was quite emotional. Finally, I figured out what was going on, and I said, "Do you think I am here to fight you?" Immediately tears started to stream down my face, I couldn't believe what was going on! He answered, "Aren't you?" "No!" I said emphatically, "What's wrong with you? What happened to you, Dad?" And I wept and wept. This man was no longer my dad. My dad was now gone and this bitter and angry person was all that was left. I couldn't see Jesus in him at all. It was so sad. Roger became very nervous seeing my tears and he practically ran up to his house.

He yelled back from the door, "When you are ready to hear what I have to say about your brother and your mother you can come over my house, until then, leave me alone." I told him I couldn't hear him talk badly about my mother and brother. And so he slammed the door. That was the last time any of us kids saw our dad for seven years.

Shortly after that event, mom got pregnant out of wedlock, and then again a year later. Suddenly I was a 24-year-old man with a baby sister and a baby brother. My soon- to-be new step dad, was only 11 years older than me, it was a nightmare. I couldn't believe it was happening. My mother's soon-to-be husband ended up working for me. I actually liked him, but it was strange to watch all this happening; and there was nothing that I could do about it. I felt so so sorry for my mother. It would be her fourth marriage. I prayed and prayed that it would work out for her.

I have always loved my mother. I like to think that I understand her. Her childhood was so tough, and then the religious stuff she learned actually kept her in bondage for the better part of her life. It was always easy to forgive her. I just wanted her to be happy. She was just a girl, a grown up girl who wanted to be loved but men kept letting her down, husband after husband, pastor after pastor, man after man. Mom just needed to feel safe; but so many of these men kept convincing her that there is no place where she is protected. Like so many of us, she has long lived in fear. She was a victim; no doubt.

There is so much I could write about what all the church people did surrounding my parent's divorce, and then even worse, what happened when she got pregnant. Elders from the church wanted her to divorce my dad, and those same elders tried to talk her into getting an abortion when she ended up pregnant. I could write volumes about the offenses inflicted on my family by the religious establishment over the years. I'm not upset with them but I am clearly stating that what they did was wrong. I guess it's all they know: they know how to be religious; no one ever taught them how to love.

At her wedding I was beyond emotional. I showed up something like an hour late and I missed the whole ceremony. I felt bad about it, sure, but I was just too overwhelmed. This was my precious mother, and I wanted her to finally be happy. I had a hard time believing that this man would be the one to bring my mother into the fullness of Christ and help her to feel safe. Sure I liked him but I couldn't see them as a good fit together. I approached my mom and her new husband at the top of the hill where they married. Richard, my mentor, married them. Richard saw that we needed to be alone. He really knew how to make some incredible moments happen. The three of us were standing there alone, as the rest of the wedding party went down to the reception at their house.

So we were alone on top of that mountain as the sun was setting off in the distance. It was quite a memorable scene. I apologized for being late. My mother looked so beautiful. Her husband looked like a male model out of a magazine. I put my right arm around my mom and my left arm around her husband, and wept as I prayed, "Lord," it was very hard to push the words through the tears, "Do whatever you must, to keep them together . . ." As the Holy Spirit of God dumped on us the three of us wept. We stood there quietly for a few moments, watching the sun go down. In my heart I continued to pray, "Help them Lord! Do a great miracle. Keep them together!"

I was nearly 27 years old. God had healed huge portions of my heart and was continuing to bring me into the Liberty in Christ. I was being set free from all kinds of broken things I sometimes did, and set free from all kinds of iniquity that held me, as if in a prison. I had a new relationship with my dad. Many of the people who were unhealthy for me were out of my life. I had several mentors that I met regularly with, and my business life was soaring. Things couldn't have been going any better for me.

Even with all the heartache those were some really incredible years!

$$\Delta \quad \Omega$$

I was extremely busy with business during those years. I started a publication in 2002 that started to explode. In 2004 that business went from printing two magazines per month to twelve across five U.S. states. It was an exciting time of life. I also started a production company with some friends, and we were filming a documentary about natural health cancer cures. I still had my mortgage company and all things were flourishing. I bought a web and software development company and watched as I was about to become very rich.

But something else was happening during those years. I was falling in love with God like never before. I saw His goodness and His mercy like I could never have imagined. People had to know about this God, I often thought. I can't be the only one to know His love. I started to tell people the good news again, "Jesus never started a religion. He wants to be our Father and our God, forever. He wants to take care of us and lead us unto life and life everlasting!"

I started a bible study at a local coffee house, and every Sunday we would gather informally. God was with us every time. I have many stories of the miracles God did in ministering to His people while we were there. My favorite story is the day the part-owner of *Girls-Gone-Wild* showed up. He didn't know me or any of us, he just saw us all sitting there and he said, "Something told him to come be with us at the table."

We sat there for an hour getting to know him and hearing his stories. Finally, he wanted help with his daughters. He told us all about the trouble he had been having with them. I explained spiritual things to him; how the sins of the fathers are passed on to the children, unless there is something to break the curse. He was over six feet tall, very muscular, bald and definitely the driven *type 'A'* personality, but he wept as we prayed for him, while the Holy Spirit came upon him; comforting him. He testified that he was going to give his life to Jesus as he left that day. I never saw him again.

I traveled a lot in 2004. And on these trips I began to see the power of God working through my life. One time, in Puerto Rico, I was up well into the night preaching to a friend of mine, Robert, and his older brother, Veny, about Jesus. They were both catholic and businessmen. They didn't seem to know the Bible very well. I shared with them many scriptures on salvation, proving that man and his religion does not have the power to save, but Jesus does. I don't think they had ever heard before what I was sharing that night. Veny and I were up until 2 or 3 in the morning.

The next day we got up early to go Marlin fishing. On the way to the boat he and his brother started to chide me, saying, "Hey Robert, why don't you pray that you catch a Marlin?" They were very sarcastic, but I took the opportunity anyway. I said, "Okay, pull the car over." And I prayed. It was a simple prayer, "Lord thank you for letting me catch a Marlin and show these guys that you are alive." Everyone was quiet for sometime after that. I guess they didn't expect me to pray.

The whole day fishing went by ... and no Marlin for Robert. Then the Captain of the sport fishing boat explained that we needed to head back to the dock. They agreed to keep the fishing lines in the water on the way back. We only had fifteen minutes left of fishing when, "Wham!" A Marlin jumped out of the water, caught on one of our lines! I fought him for forty-five minutes, and when we got him to the boat it turned out that it was a white Marlin. The Captain of the boat had never seen one before with his own eyes, they were so rare. We took pictures and let the amazing, rare fish go.

Everyone was blown away by what the Lord had done. Those business guys came over to me and said, "Robert do you want to know why we were kidding you like that in the car?" I said, "Sure." They explained, "It isn't Marlin season. So we were just playing with you. We didn't expect you to pray like that.

You caught the rarest Marlin in the water, when it wasn't even Marlin season! God did a great miracle!" I was blown away. God is amazing. He can do anything! That day God wanted to show two businessmen that He is Alive and He hears His children when they cry out to Him.

There are many more stories of the things the Lord and I were doing together during those years. I met amazing people, Kofi Anan (while he was the Secretary General of the UN), many actors, other famous people, all kinds of incredible doctors, and one of my friends was running for president of an African nation. I was on an amazing adventure with God to say the least. But I was changing all over again.

The businessman in me was departing and the desire to serve God and minister His kingdom was taking over. I prayed and asked the Lord if I could leave that life and just go to serve Him. I prayed this often throughout 2004. I just wanted to be wherever I would be of the most use to the Lord. I expressed all these thoughts to Him in prayer.

In December 2004 I was invited to speak publicly in Tucson, Arizona. I was the key note speaker at a Chamber of Commerce event. I had thirty to forty-five minutes to speak, but I just didn't want to talk about making money. I was supposed to talk about marketing and the "secret of my success" at such a young age, but all I wanted to talk about was Jesus. Reluctantly, I stood behind the microphone and tried to talk.

If you know me, you know that I usually don't have a problem finding something to talk about. But I just couldn't do it. I tried to talk about money and making more money, but my heart just wasn't in it. Finally, I said, "Have you guys ever seen a movie where the main character has a life changing moment in front of a room, maybe while he is speaking? Well, this isn't a movie but I am having that life changing moment right now, in front of you all. You see, I have always wanted to serve God with my life. I never really wanted to be a business guy. So I just decided I am going to leave it all now. I'm going to go and serve the Lord. I hope you all have the courage to follow your hearts too. Good evening." Again there was no applause and I practically ran off the stage!

I went and hid myself from everyone, even several of my employees who were there with me. I just wanted to be alone. I went to a bar and found a spot where no one would be able to find me, and I prayed, "I want out Lord! I want to come and serve you! Can I leave all this now?" He said, "You can leave this behind, but I have one condition." I said, "Yes Lord?" He said, "You can never worry about money again. You have to trust that I will take care of you." That was good news to me. I agreed and made up my mind. I was done with business.

I returned to L.A. and started making my way out of business immediately. It would take a full year, but I did it. I was totally out of business by the end of 2005 . . . never to return.

That's when my Father started to make a minister of the kingdom of God out of me.

And my life changed all over again!

Chapter 5

I have been kicked out of several churches over the years. One time I was weeping at the altar, praying for people in the church during a prayer service, and the pastor said I was being a distraction. He sent his elders over to have me escorted out, and I was told not to return. Days later I was on the phone with the pastor, trying to make sense of what happened. The pastor told me in his forty years of pastoring he had never before seen anything like this. I asked him, "You have never seen someone weeping and interceding before at the altar of a church?" I was in absolute shock and awe. He had come out of the Jesus Movement of the 70's so he must have seen people crying out to God, I thought. How was it possible that he had become so hardhearted?

This pastor continued to get more and more upset with me on the phone, demanding an apology of me. I asked him what I did wrong. He insisted that going to the altar during a prayer service was out of order, and that I would not be allowed back at his church unless I apologized. All his elders agreed, saying practically nothing the whole conversation. He felt justified even though one of the people I was praying and weeping for at the altar was his own daughter who had recently been diagnosed with cancer. I have many of these strange stories from within the religious institutions.

There was another time a demon possessed woman was sitting in front of me at a church service. There was an evangelist preaching then and there was a special anointing in the room for deliverance, many of us could feel it. I motioned to an usher sitting near to me about this woman to keep his eyes on

her. He knew me a little bit and he agreed. When the evangelist made an altar call she went up front, but there was no one
there to pray with her. Everyone else had a person standing
with them to pray for them personally, except for her. I asked
the usher what I should do? He asked if I wanted to go up and
pray with her? I nodded, yes.

While I was going to pray for her the associate pastor saw
me. I followed the prayer team back into the prayer room, but
she was given someone else to pray with. So I ended up just
leaving. Moments later that associate pastor tracked me down
to yell at me. He was very irritated that I would go and pray with
someone since I had not been 'approved' by their prayer team. I
tried to explain to him that I got permission from the usher, but
he would not listen to me, he just kept coming down harder and
harder on me, telling me that I was out of order and must submit
to authority.

I saw the usher and I pulled him over, but this pastor would
not stop. I saw the senior pastor who also knew me and I pulled
him into the conversation. The senior pastor did not know what
to do. He was also in shock. But even realizing how wrong this
associate pastor was, he would not correct him or bring peace
to the situation. That's when the associate pastor started hollering at me that if I didn't leave the church immediately he would
have me forcibly escorted out. I literally had to laugh. The whole
thing was so ridiculous.

I said, "Do you not understand that if the Holy Spirit tells
me to go and pray for someone, I am a minister and I am well
within Biblical guidelines to go and pray for her. The fact that I
got permission tells you that I gave respect to your way of doing
things. You are way out of line." To this day they have never
admitted any wrong-doing.

The worst part about this story is that a new believer,
Luke, was standing with me watching all this happen, but these
pastors just couldn't control themselves. That associate pastor
literally would have punched me in the face if it hadn't been
for the senior pastor standing there with us. He could hardly

control himself. It was alarming to see how badly the leadership of these religious institutions had fallen.

Who is in charge of the Church anyway, men or Jesus?

Δ   Ω

It was 2005, and God was changing me into a minister. I was so broken and sinful that it did not happen overnight. But the Lord in His gentle way was changing me. From 2005 to 2008, He kept taking me on these adventures. I was being changed, being made more into His image every day. He was opening the scriptures to me and helping me to see His kingdom. I have enough stories to share from these years that I could write an entire book just about the beginning of ministry.

God has somehow put me in these incredible places, with these incredible people so often. I am just a kid from Detroit. I don't come from anywhere, but somehow God has continually put me in front of people with position and clout, and in many amazing places. In Bible College I met Vice President Al Gore, he pinched my cheek and told me that I was good looking. It was weird. I guess he was trying to be nice. I told you how I met the Secretary General of the United Nations, Kofi Annan. He was an intimidating character, so strong for a man of shorter stature. I met John McCain when he was running for President. At times I felt like Forest Gump. Remember how he always ended up in these incredible places? I think maybe the Lord kept doing this on my travels to show me that He has the power to put us anywhere He wants to put us.

By late 2005 I got rid of my apartment and almost all my possessions. I sold my car and gave away or sold everything I had in storage. By the end of 2005, everything I owned fit into two suitcases! I was totally free of encumbrances. In one year I went from being on the stage asking God if I could leave everything, to being nearly flat broke with everything I owned in the world fitting into two suitcases. Life sure had changed.

I went broke because when I went to go and sell that publication this businessman I was associated with found out how much the company was worth and he tried to steal it in court. He pretended to be a friend and faked his desire to help me. He called himself a 'Christian' and told me he vacationed every year with his pastor. Whatever. He was a thief. He did everything he could to steal the company. The whole company ended up bankrupt by 2006.

I could write another book about all the horrors I suffered while in business. And most of them came at the hands of Christian brothers; I had hired many brothers to come and work for me from church. I have lots and lots of stories about that too. But it's not worth writing about. It was the end of 2005 and I was completely done. I just wanted to go and preach the gospel. It didn't matter to me that the company folded and I never got all that money. I was free; finally free!

God gave me another new mentor that year. He was an eighty three year old World War II Veteran named Tom. Tom was a precious elder in the Lord and Tom suffered at the time from dementia. I would run into Tom at the coffee shop from time to time and we became close friends. I will never forget the first day we met.

I was just beginning to write my thoughts down about "Jesus not starting a Religion" in my journal. All of this was so fresh inside of me and one day this lovely old man sat down next to me and introduced himself, "Hi, I am Tom. I saw your bible out and I thought to come and introduce myself." We spoke for quite a while and he gave me a copy of his testimony as he left to return home. I read it as soon as I received it. Tom's story moved me mightily!

Tom's testimony began telling about how father had gone broke in the stock market crash of '29 and his mother, beyond distraught from the loss, killed herself, Tom was only 9 years old. Tom's story read like the script of a movie and quite fitting since Tom had fifty-some-odd years working behind a camera in the film industry in L.A. As I got to the part where Tom wrote about meeting his beloved wife, Mary, I couldn't hold back the tears. It was so beautiful and innocent, Tom's testimony of how Jesus brought Mary into his life. They were married shortly after his return from WWII and they rented a chicken coop just outside of L.A. for their first home.

Tom became my new very best friend. We would spend hours and hours together at that coffee shop discussing scripture and Tom would tell me his life's stories. He wasn't perfect and he never pretended to be. He told me some of his failures too. He was an alcoholic at one point in his life but then he found Jesus! And everything changed for Tom just like life had changed for me when I found Jesus! God did something incredible in my heart while I was with Tom. It's hard to explain quickly but Tom showed me the power of the simplicity of loving someone.

Tom with dementia encouraged me to start trusting the Lord again in ways I hadn't done since I was in Bible College. Tom would encourage me about my writing. He would often show up with scriptures God had given him for me the night before as he prayed for me. (I had never met anyone who had ever prayed into the night for me!) Tom was very simple in his faith. And simply the love of God was all that he needed to win this impressionable young me back to living by faith! It was Tom who first inspired me to write a book!

After Tom six other people who did not know each other, told me that I should write a book. Could the Lord have shouted it any louder? I would have had to be a fool to miss what the Lord was saying. When I prayed, "What do I write about?" There was only one, clear answer, "Jesus didn't start a Religion."

Probably in April or May 2005 I started writing this book. About the same time I started writing, God healed Tom of dementia! One day I showed up, I hadn't seen Tom in a few months and he reported to me that the dementia had gone into remission! It was another Jesus miracle. Jesus healed my dear friend Tom! (Tom is about 93 years old as of the writing of this book. He tells me that he is still waiting to go to heaven. Mary is faithfully by his side. They have been married some 60+ years now!) I have loved Tom since the day I met him!

Then by 2006 I was writing this book full time, traveling around and sharing whatever the Lord gave me. It has taken all these years to discern the message the Lord was revealing. It has truly been a journey that Tom greatly helped to inspire. (Thank you Tom, I love you very much.) God has clearly had a plan from the start!

Δ   Ω

One day I was on a train headed back to Los Angeles from Eugene, Oregon. I had met this homosexual man and I was ministering to him about God's love. He knew much of the Bible, he was raised in church. He was in the fashion industry. He was clearly a very intelligent, talented and successful guy. It was a 20-something hour train ride and for the first three or four hours of it we discussed life and the things of God. He was surprisingly open to talking about Jesus.

We were hungry and moved to the café area in the train and kept talking. Then a few other guys joined in our discussion and a few others. As we continued, eventually there were 11 or 12 of us guys all discussing things of the scriptures! It was incredible. This Israeli soldier asked the best questions out of everybody there. He was on vacation, touring the U.S. He wanted to know everything about "Jesus not starting a religion," it was very interesting to him. He had never heard of such things before.

I explained, "Jesus was a Jew. He never stood up and said, 'Hey everyone, we aren't going to be Jews anymore, we are going to be Christians'. Jesus never built anything, He never created a new name for Himself and His followers to go by, and He never created a hierarchy of command before He left. Jesus lived by the Spirit of His Father every day, loving the people that God put in front of Him. He was less interested in the masses, but much more interested in the individuals around Him. Religion today does it almost exactly the opposite. Religion is concerned with the masses; religion wants to establish things on this earth while Jesus was concerned about establishing things on earth as they are in heaven. The Israeli Soldier told me that *he had never heard anything like this before*. He was very interested and kept the conversation going for several hours. All the others guys, for the most part, were listening in.

While I was talking (and it has been said that I can talk pretty loud), there was this woman, at least 70 years old, sitting toward the front of the café, maybe 3 or 4 booths away from us, she was listening intently to every word I was saying. I noticed her on several occasions making eye contact with me. It seemed that she wanted to meet me. Finally, as my time with "the guys" ended, I went over and introduced myself to her. She was a little timid, but welcomed me into her booth.

It turned out that this woman had experienced a life that very few people would ever live. She was a world renowned concert pianist and played the piano for five U.S. Presidents. She was personal friends with Billy Graham and many others of the upper echelon of the 'church world'. As she told me her life's story I was in awe. She had been married to a very prominent evangelist in the 50s, who had become homosexual while they were married. He was cheating on her with men for most of her marriage. She told me all kinds of horror stories about many of the things that go on in the world of organized Christianity that are obviously never publicized.

She invited me to come to Arkansas and meet some of her friends. She was excited about the book and said that she could get it published for me. I told her about all the things that the Lord was showing me and she was very eager to help. Dr. Jack Hayford, my former pastor from Church on the Way, picked her up from the train station in a limousine. I was so excited! Was this my big shot into Christian stardom? I told my mother about everything that happened when I arrived at her house.

A few months after that train ride I was in Arkansas. The piano player knew everyone. She introduced me to a woman who was the traveling companion of Corrie ten Boom the last ten years of her life. She introduced me to publishers and many other authors and who's who types throughout the Christendom. I was on the phone one day with the wife of Bob Pierce, the founder of World Vision. On and on it went for weeks, while I was with the concert pianist. But something was not sitting right with my spirit, as exciting as it all was.

When I was discussing my publishing contract with these Christian publishers I was appalled by their business-attitude. Maybe I was a bit naïve? But they talked about my book in mere business terms. What I was doing for the Lord and the very important message I had been given was never discussed. Rather, it was how the book would sell and where I would preach and the length of the book tour I was willing to do; those were the topics of conversation. The President of one of the largest Christian publishing companies told me that they do not publish prophetic works like I had written. He seemed offended by the audacity of my writing style and the boldness of the message.

My innocent and young mind could not conceive that this was the *real world* of Christianity for which Christ had given His life some two-thousand years before. So many of these Christian men of position were like every day businessmen, just like the bankers, stock brokers, real estate agents and lawyers that I had known so well in years past. Literally, not one of them wanted to pray with me over the phone. Not one of them gave me any encouragement about serving the Lord, or words of wisdom for a young man, guiding me along the way. Nope. It was business as usual and I just so happened to be the topic of conversation that day. I was grieved to say the least.

One rather large publishing company wanted to sign me to a book contract; however they wanted me on a 24-month book tour. I was excited, but still rather defensive after all I had just seen. I asked them a lot of questions about how the contract would work and what I came to realize was that I was signing my rights away. In their minds they were helping me to market the book, but in my mind I was losing my ability to go where the Spirit would lead me and do as the Spirit was directing. When I asked if I would have any control over where I did or did not preach, the answer was clearly—No.

I could not get comfortable with all this; in no way was it acceptable! I had to get away to pray and ask the Lord what to do. I borrowed one of their cars. I went on a trip to see an Archeologist friend of mine who lived only a state away. This archeologist had been a part of finding some of the most amazing things from the Bible: the actual Mount Sinai, Gomorrah and the other cities destroyed near Sodom, Noah's Ark, and several other incredible things. I got to his place and started talking with him about letting me get him on Oprah's television show.

My brother had dated this girl who worked in Chicago with some of Oprah's people. She worked at a big Public Relations firm that often worked with Oprah. I told my archeologist friend about my connection in Chicago and he said, "I will never get on Oprah. She doesn't want to hear anything about what I have to say. But if you want, go ahead and see what you can do." I was in the car the next day driving to Chicago.

My brother's ex-girlfriend repeated almost word for word what my archeologist friend had said, "No way will Oprah want him on her show. She doesn't believe in these things at all." She encouraged me to see the sights while I was in Chicago, and told me about a major Christian university downtown. She said I should go and check it out. I decided I would go.

When I arrived at that university I was horrified by the cold and callused attitude everyone seemed to have around that place. I was there for two hours, and the whole time I was rejected and treated like garbage, for no reason. I went to introduce myself to a table of students who were having a conversation about Jesus, and one of them literally looked at me and said, "Can't you see we are having a private conversation here and you are interrupting us?" I responded, "You are in a public place talking about Jesus and I am a brother in the Lord." They somewhat politely asked me to leave. I had at least three doors slammed in my face, and more than five people did not greet me back when I said, hello to them. I am not exaggerating; it was even worse than that.

What set me off more than anything was the life-sized statue of the man for whom the college was named, in the library. *"Who are they worshipping here?"* I thought to myself, horrified and offended. My time there continued to go downhill. I prayed, "Lord, I don't even think they know Jesus here? But what can I do about it?" The Lord responded in that way He often does, "What do you want to do?" I said, "Me? I don't know but I'd like to do something." The Lord responded, "Are you willing to go to jail for me?"

Now when the Lord asks you a question like, "Are you willing to go to jail for me?" You had better be very careful what you say next. I thought about this question for upwards of 30 minutes until I finally said, "I am willing to go to jail for you, but only if it works. If people get saved I will gladly suffer for you, Lord." The Lord promised that it would work and He directed me outside. I saw three students standing in the courtyard and the Lord told me to testify about all I had seen that morning.

The three of them were just as rude as all the rest, completely uninterested in what I was saying, and arguing that maybe there was something wrong with me. I reasoned with them, "But I have done nothing wrong. I am a brother in the Lord and I have been treated horribly the two hours or more that I've been here." But they simply didn't care about what I was saying.

As we were talking more students joined the conversation and then even more until finally there was a crowd gathered around me and I was full-on preaching. Within fifteen minutes or so, there were hundreds of students gathered outside and listening to me proclaiming, "Jesus didn't start a religion"! The Spirit of God had come upon me in great power, and I was declaring the kingdom of God with great boldness. It was amazing. I had never felt the Spirit like that before!

A security guard came over to me and told me to leave. I told him that I was on public property and that he had no right to force me to leave. He called the cops and lied to them and told them that I was suicidal. He smiled this evil smile and said,

"You are going to leave whether you like it or not." I didn't let him steal my focus and I kept on preaching.

There was one young guy, practically with tears in his eyes, who said, "What do you want us to do? What is God asking of us?" I responded, "Finally, someone with a heart. Finally someone who loves God!" I told him, "I want you to leave these bricks, these buildings and these institutions. Go out into the world and love them. Show them Jesus! Learn to minister the kingdom of God and then come back here and teach all these friends of yours to do the same. This gospel is a gospel of love, go and love the world!" He wept quite emotionally as I encouraged him in front of the whole crowd.

By the time the cops showed up there must have been three hundred people gathered and listening to me. The students were now shouting profanities at me and telling me that they were going to hurt me. I told them, "Can't you see that you are proving my point as you are threatening me and cursing me?" The cops asked me to leave with them. But I told them that I was within my rights to speak. "This is a public assembly," I told them. They urged me to come down, but I responded, "If you would give me five or ten minutes to finish I will come with you." But after hearing this they grabbed me and threw me on the ground, like I was a terrorist or something.

As I hit the ground I looked into the eyes of that young guy, the one I had been talking with earlier, and I saw him weeping, I said, "Don't weep for me. Weep for yourselves. Weep for the Church. It's all broken. We need Jesus to fix it! Only Jesus can do this!" And the cops hauled me off into some room inside of the school and started to interrogate me.

I was surrounded by something like ten police officers and they started searching my things and asking me questions. While I was responding the craziest thing happened. I don't remember the question they had asked me, but suddenly this demon took over this one cop and he charged me from the far end of the room! Shouting, "I'm going to f***'n kill you!" He pulled out his night-stick and was about to strike me in the face when two other cops grabbed him and pulled him outside! It was crazy!

The whole room went nuts. Everyone was trying to figure out what happened. "What made him so mad?" They asked each other. And it was then that the officer in charge realized something *not-of-this-world* was going on. He looked at me and said, "You know what happened, don't you?" I said, "Yes." Suddenly his attitude changed completely and he was softer and kind to me. He said, "We can't just let you go? But I'm not going to arrest you." I was shocked! Did he know God? I wondered.

They ended up taking me to a mental hospital and telling them that I was suicidal. I told the nurse that they never heard me say that, and that I was not suicidal but the nurse responded, "If the cops bring you here we have to check you out." I was released seven hours later after they played all these mind games with me to try to determine whether or not I was crazy. It is frightening what goes on in that place they call a hospital it's enough to drive anyone mad. I was overwhelmed to say the least, but then just as suddenly as it all began, it was all over.

It was two o'clock in the morning and I was wandering the streets of inner city Chicago, trying to find the parking garage where I had put the pianist's car I had borrowed. I could hardly believe all that had happened throughout that day. I was emotional to say the least. But the Lord was near; comforting me.

A year or so after Chicago, the Lord did an incredible miracle, confirming that He did amazing things through this event. I will tell that story in a chapter or two.

After I left Chicago I drove to Atlanta to spend time with a good friend of mine. I had to get alone for a while. I was very tired and emotionally drained. I had to pray about what I would do with this book contract. I had to hear from the Lord. All the while my heart was hurting for the brokenness of the church. It was all a little much to handle. The problem was so much bigger than I had realized!

But God was with me all the way; giving me grace.

Chapter 6

It was very hard to imagine that God didn't want me to get a publishing contract. I seemed like I had my new dreams on a silver platter just waiting for me to sign, but it all felt wrong. It was hard to figure out why I couldn't get comfortable. The enemy was very tricky. I remember, he kept whispering things in my ear like, "you are just afraid of success", and "you self-destruct every time you get close to really making it." He is very cunning. But no matter what was happening in my thoughts I just couldn't find peace in moving ahead.

I was living outside of Atlanta with Ed, a dear friend of mine. Ed and I had previously been in mortgage business together. Ed is a man of God. We called him, "The Watchman" because he wakes up very early every morning and intercedes for the kingdom of God. I hung out with Ed and his family for some two months as I thought and prayed about what I would do. I couldn't find peace. I couldn't find peace in saying yes or no. I just couldn't figure out why the Lord would want me to pass on spreading this great message He gave me. It was a very difficult decision for me.

One day walking out of Ed's office there was this man who seemed to be homeless staring right at me. It was as if he knew me? I walked towards him and he said, "Hey". There wasn't anyone else around. It seemed almost like he was waiting for me. I said, "Hi. Is there anything I can do for you?" He simply said, "No." Then all the sudden I found myself inviting him to go and have coffee with me. I asked him if he needed any money. He said, "I don't need any money but you can buy me a coffee if you want."

It was very strange, the whole meeting. We got to the coffee shop and ordered our drinks. He said I could buy him whatever I was drinking. And then he followed me over to a chair and sat down with me. I'm not sure that I intended to sit down with him but there he was across from me nonetheless. Then it got even stranger because he started asking me questions, saying "So what's going on with you?" It was so odd having this man, who seemed so needy asking me about my life so I just had to tell him what was going on. I told him about my book and about the people who were helping me to publish, I told him about my desire to serve God and about how I just couldn't get comfortable making a decision one way or the other. He just sat there asking very good questions and listening intently. I felt like I was in a counseling session.

What made it even more odd was that he did not talk about himself at all. I tried to find out who he was and where he came from, but he would respond with these vague answers, like, "I'm not from around here." But he wouldn't offer up where he was from. I asked him about his family and got the same vague responses. He would then turn the conversation back to me. Who was this man? I thought. But he seemed to be genuinely concerned about me so I kept talking.

By the end of the conversation an hour later he said, "It sounds to me like these people aren't interested in what you want to accomplish. It sounds like they are a huge distraction. It sounds to me like they are using you for some reason." The moment he said that it's like a light went off inside of me, *that's it!* I realized *it's the enemy trying to get me off track: he is trying to get me off of my purpose in Christ!* And I remembered how Jesus was tempted in the wilderness and part of that temptation was to make a deal with the devil. The devil said, "If you bow down and worship me I will give you all the kingdoms of the world." But Jesus did not falter and He rebuked the devil and the devil left Him. (Matthew 4)

Suddenly it was all so clear! God did not want me publishing with them. It was just that simple. God had another, better plan, and I needed to rest in that. We finished our coffee and he walked me outside. As we were saying goodbye he blessed me. It was so odd to receive a blessing from a homeless man. He said, "You are going to do well in your life. It seems to me that God is with you. Don't worry about anything. God is on your side." And just like that he turned and walked away. He never even told me his name. I wonder if I will ever know this side of heaven who that man was?

I believe with all my heart that heaven is much closer than we realize. God sends messengers to us we when need them, nothing has changed, God is the same yesterday, today and forever. He is very close, much closer than we know.

Δ   Ω

It's a very long story but when I finally made it back to Arkansas, those *Christian* people turned on me when I told them that I needed time to before I would be ready to publish. In an instant I was rejected and out of their lives forever. To this day they have never responded to an email or a phone call. That concert pianist was one day crying and telling me that she was going to introduce me to the world, but then after I told her I was not ready and that I needed some time, she kicked me out of her house with nowhere to go. Now I do have to admit, she had introduced me to a young friend of hers that she was hoping I would marry, but the Lord wasn't in any of that. This was all a life that these people were creating for me; this was not the life that God was giving me. But the Lord wanted to teach me, He was teaching me to trust His voice over the voice of man. He was teaching me in a way that a Father would teach His son.

After I was booted out of her house I had nowhere to go. I was flat broke, and I didn't know anyone in that town, except for a young Christian guy I met once at a book store, while studying one afternoon. I had his number so I called him. His name was Casey. I explained to him that I needed a place to stay for the night and he very reluctantly agreed, Casey said, "I don't know how my roommate will like this, but for one night it's okay." The next day he left for work and I was alone with my rejection and sorrow.

I couldn't even pray that day. I turned on his PlayStation or whatever game machine he had and played video games all day. What kind a man of God was I? I had just preached this powerful message in Chicago and almost got arrested—I had been traveling all over America for years, preaching the things God gave me, but the "man of God" was reduced to just playing video games all day. I felt unbelievably hurt, lost and forgotten. I could have sat at that television and played those games for days and been completely content, never leaving Casey's house.

But then Casey came home. He slammed the door open, pointed at me and yelled out, "Now I know you are a real man of God!" I'm sure I had potato chips all over my shirt, my eyes were probably bloodshot from playing those games all day nonstop, and there were many empty packages of Top Ramen tossed throughout the kitchen as Casey proclaimed my authenticity. He explained, "I was working (at Best Buy) today and this 70- or 80-something year-old woman came up to me and said that she knew that I was a believer. She said she could see it in my eyes! I agreed and told her that she was right. Then she put a $2,000 check made out to cash in my hands! You are a real man of God! I'm taking care of everything! God just gave us two grand buddy! Let's go shopping! What do you need!?"

My mood obviously immediately changed. I was also happy to learn that I was still in God's favor. Casey was maybe 19 years old and $2,000 is a lot of money when you are only 19. I am sure no stranger had ever given him $2,000 before. It was another Jesus miracle. I badly needed a boost of the old-morale. It always feels good to know that God has your back.

I left Arkansas and the south shortly thereafter and did not look back. I was leaving so much hurt behind. Maybe they felt hurt and let down too? I'm sure. But what could I do? I had to obey the leading of the Lord. You could say I left Arkansas with my tail between my legs. I did not feel victorious. I felt like I had just barely escaped a terrible trap that nearly slammed shut around my leg. I didn't have a clue what I would do next, but back to Los Angeles I went.

Δ Ω

I ended up moving in with these Baptist guys. They were going to a rather famous Bible College outside of Los Angeles. The third in command at the Bible College owned the house. He rented out rooms to many of the students. I was introduced to him by my friend Elijah, who also lived in the house, and he agreed to rent me a room. There must have been nine or ten of us living in a five bedroom, ranch style home. I had no idea what I was in for next.

One day I was telling stories about my life to the Baptist Bible College students when they suddenly got bothered about my remarks with regards to the Holy Spirit and the baptism of fire. Several of them, maybe four or five, teamed up against me to battle out the doctrine of the baptism of the Holy Ghost. I really do not like to fight over scripture, *not even a little bit*, so I tried my best to defuse the situation. Finally, I ended the argument with, "Whatever you guys want to believe is your choice, but I want to give you a warning. The only unpardonable sin is blasphemy of the Holy Spirit. So whatever you go on to do with your lives just be careful when dealing with things surrounding God's Holy Ghost." They remained angry and continued to try to argue, but I wouldn't debate them anymore.

It was clear that I had bothered the peace of the house, so the prominent figure at the Bible College called me and scheduled a meeting with us all at the house. I thought he was coming to make peace. But when he arrived and started talking, it was abundantly clear that he had no intention of making peace. He started in on me in front of all the other guys who lived there. He said, "There is no such thing as the baptism of the Holy Spirit!" The conversation got heated and even though I tried my best to keep everyone calm, emotions were already flying out of control!

All of the sudden the 60-something-year-old, third-in-command of the prestigious Bible College started to charge at me! I couldn't believe it! I guess a demon had control of him too! Let me paint a more detailed picture for you; that man was over 6 feet 4 inches tall and probably 260+ lbs! He was like a giant and so I ran away from him as fast as I could. I ended up running around the couch and was sort of laughing in unbelief that this old man was so out of control: The Vice President of a Bible College? I couldn't help but chuckle a little. Finally, after a couple laps around the couch, the Spirit of God came upon me and I pointed at him with authority and shouted his name and said, "You need to go outside and get a hold of yourself. You are out of control!" Suddenly he sort of came too and realized what he was doing and went outside to calm himself. Everyone in the house was totally silent. None of us could believe what had just happened?

Moments later he came back in. He seemed to have gotten control of himself and kind of started to apologize. During his weak apology he got all worked up again and was ready to attack me a second time. When I realized that he was about to lose it a second time, I said, "Do you need to go outside again? What is wrong with you? Why can't you keep control of yourself?" It's kind of a humorous story writing it down because this man was around 60 years old and I was not even 30, but I was absolutely acting like the senior man. I couldn't believe it was happening. I packed my things and moved out that day. (My awesome Uncle Dennis came and saved me again. I should write about the several times my Uncle Dennis came and saved me. But it's a little off topic.)

I never spoke with him again except to call and tell him that I forgave him, and there is no harm done. He was still upset with me on the phone clearly but accepted my apology. His apology sounded like this, "I don't know what you did you me. I have never been so angry before in my whole life!" It was over as far as I was concerned.

I have so many wild and funny stories from my adventures with Jesus. One guy at that house was from Alaska and every time he would talk about Alaska I would get really excited. His name was Steve. Steve and I went on an adventure together; to rescue his mom from the hospital. They were trying to keep her against her will, it was nuts! But that is a whole other story, maybe for another day. But through Steve the Spirit of God was confirming that He was sending me to Alaska. Steve helped me to find a job up there working at a Christian Summer Camp. Within a month after leaving the Baptist house I was on a plane to Fairbanks, Alaska! And my adventures with Jesus continued.

Δ   Ω

I have never had a worse greeting in my life than the greeting I got from the woman who ran that summer camp. The day I arrived in Fairbanks they sent a van to pick me up at the airport. Everyone who would be working at the camp met at a church. When I met Lisa, the camp director, she literally rolled her eyes and said, "Of course you are Robert." And she refused to shake my hand as I extended it to her. To this day I don't know what she meant by that remark.

(Remember as I tell you these stories that these are all Christian *church* people.) If I haven't mentioned it yet I will mention it here; when I have made mistakes I have tended to make very big ones! I don't make a lot of small mistakes; I make a few really really big mistakes. And I met a girl at that summer camp who I fell for immediately. Oops . . . I was hired to be a camp counselor for kids and here I was flirting with disaster. Then things got even stranger.

Suzy and I got to know each other, after a week or two. I learned that she had just graduated from the same Bible College in Chicago where I had nearly been arrested. What are the odds? I was in Fairbanks Alaska with this lovely girl who just so happened to go to the college where I was nearly arrested a year earlier. It took me some time, but I finally told her the story. I told her who I was . . .

Wouldn't you know it? She was there and listening to me preach! Do you realize how far Fairbanks, Alaska is from Chicago? Or from Los Angeles? What a miracle God did in bringing both of us to that place. She told me, with shock and awe, her side of the story; witnessing me preach and declare the Word of God that day in Chicago, and then being thrown on the ground by the cops! It turned out that I did in fact make big waves that day. Praise God! I had finally got my answer! God was in fact with me. It worked, just like He had promised. The message I shared did in fact break through to their hearts!!

As things progressed at camp, Lisa's hatred towards me also progressed. Finally, one day it all came to a head. They were very angry at me for getting a coffee when I wasn't supposed to and they called the head of the board of directors to the camp for a meeting. I thought he was coming to make peace but no, again, he was coming to attack me.

This *Christian* man was so frightening! The president of the camp looked exactly like "the Uni-bomber" (if you can recall that man who bombed some building in the US, he wore a hooded sweat-shirt and dark tinted glasses, with a bushy beard, very scary looking). So there I was again in front of the firing squad. The Uni-Bomber, Lisa and her right hand guy, some 22-year-old with a large inferiority complex; I asked them, "What did I do wrong?" They were all so angry that they just started shouting about the coffee that I drank and how I have no respect for their authority. I tried to calm them down, but it wasn't happening. They wanted me to admit I was wrong for getting the coffee and admit that I was a horrible employee, etc.

I just didn't feel like being there anymore. I wasn't an employee, I was a volunteer basically working for free so I told them, "If I am such a terrible employee you should probably just let me go." That enraged them even more. I thought for sure the Uni-Bomber was going to punch me in the face. He was incredibly mad . . . *and* incredibly strange. (What President of a Bible Camp comes to a meeting wearing a hooded sweatshirt, with the hood up, and refuses to take his pitch black glasses off?)

Then it got even stranger. They called the cops! They lied to the police and said that I was a danger to the kids. They said I was a disgruntled employee and they had better come in a hurry or else I might hurt someone. I couldn't believe that this was happening. And again, in case I didn't say it clearly enough, this was a *Christian* camp that I had volunteered at . . .

I prayed and the Lord told me to leave the camp immediately. So I started to walk away. And they started hollering at me, "And where do you think you are going?" I didn't know where I was going, I was just going to leave the camp like the Lord had said. The camp was in the middle of nowhere, way out in the woods in Alaska. A land full of bears, moose and all kinds of things that can hurt you; and let me remind you that I am completely a "city-boy". After twenty minutes or so I found myself all alone down an Alaskan country road without a house or anyone in sight. I couldn't help but feel small and afraid.

The Lord assured me that He was with me. After maybe two miles I came to this house out in the middle of the woods. It was the only place nearby so I went up to the door and knocked. The owner was home. I explained to him the whole story to which he responded, "Yeah. That camp is known for being strange, kinda' like a cult." He encouraged me to go back to the camp and talk with the cops. He said, "The cops in Alaska aren't anything like the cops in L.A., they will listen to you." I was comforted to say the least and I returned to the camp. I arrived just as the police showed up.

It was just as the man had said. The cops from the start appeared to be on my side. One of them even referred to the woman, Lisa, as being totally out-of-control, and they understood that I had been the victim. They made sure I was safe to return back to the camp to retrieve all my things. The Uni-Bomber wanted to give me a ride back to the airport but I would not get in the car with him. Lisa ended up recruiting Rose, the woman in charge of the kitchen to escort me with her; and the three of us headed back to town.

Now Rose was often troubled by me too. On several occasions when I was praying at camp, Rose seemed to be bothered by me, and interrupted me a time or two. I didn't know what I had done to her? Maybe I was just too happy? But we never talked long enough for me to figure it out. Needless to say, I was not excited to be in the car with these two women for more than two hours. We all sat there completely in quiet as they drove me to town. Then out of nowhere Rose started to cry!? Lisa assumed Rose was crying because I was such a terrible person and she tried to console Rose.

But then Rose burst out, "No! It's wrong," she said, "what we have done to him is wrong, Lisa! Robert has done nothing since he arrived here but love the children and pray for everyone; and we all hated him for it! It's wrong Lisa! We are supposed to be Christians, he is our young brother and we have treated him terribly for no reason!" Rose wept and wept. Lisa tried to defend herself and the actions of the Uni-Bomber but Rose wouldn't listen. Rose said even louder, "That's it Lisa! I quit! If you can't see that what you have done to this man is wrong, then I can't, in good conscience, work with you anymore! When we take Robert back to town you can turn around and take me to get my things also. I'm leaving too!" Lisa was shocked and started to plead with Rose, saying, "Rose, how can you not see how horrible he is?" And Rose got even more upset, "What has he done to any of you?" She shouted! And then Rose remained quiet for a while. Lisa was so mad at me she wouldn't say a word when she dropped me off in downtown Fairbanks.

The Lord was certainly showing me the brokenness of the *religion* called, *Christianity*. He was showing me the intensity of the problem that is against us.

I saw firsthand this religion destroying the work of God . . .

Chapter 7

Rose asked me if I really wanted to leave town. Nothing inside of me wanted to go. Lisa was doing her best to kick me out of Fairbanks but I didn't feel it was God's will for me to leave just yet. I told Rose, "I don't know Rose. I would like to pray and ask the Lord what His will is." Rose said, "I will pay for you to stay in a hotel just don't stay longer than a week, okay?" I was in tears again. I couldn't believe how God had turned this woman's heart towards me. (Rose became my friend and we have remained friends to this day!)

They dropped me off at this hotel and Rose gave them her credit card. I promised Rose that the Lord would give me some direction within the next day because I didn't want to spend all her money. In no way was Rose wealthy or anything. That night I refused to watch television or dwell too much on all the drama that had just unfolded. I prayed that God would forgive all these people, and I asked Him if I should stay or go. The Lord asked me, "What do you want to do?" I said, "I feel like I should stay for some reason." And I knew for certain that the Lord was with me.

I didn't know a single person in town so the next morning when I awoke I didn't know what I would do about staying in Alaska. I had a small check from my per diem at the camp that I needed to cash, because that was all the money I had in the whole world. The front desk told me about a supermarket that would cash my check, but it would be a long walk. I started down the street, praying the whole way, wondering if the Lord was going to do something to keep me there.

I walked past a church but the Lord said don't go inside. I looked across the street there was another church a little further down the road. The Lord said, "Go inside of that church. If they greet you and welcome you then stay in town, but *if you are rejected again wipe the dust off your feet and leave* Fairbanks." It seemed like simple enough instructions.

When I got inside of that church there happened to be a lot of people there. It was Worship Band rehearsal! I walked in and two men greeted me. One turned out to be the pastor. He was very kind, and interested in who I was. I told him that I was on my way to cash a check and he offered to give me a ride. Kindness! (Oh, how badly I needed a little kindness that day.) The pastor was from Los Angeles of all places, and invited me to stay for their service that evening. After we cashed my check I was in such a good mood that I decided to buy several, three-foot long sub sandwiches and chips, for the church to eat for dinner. The pastor enjoyed my thoughtful gesture.

When the church service began, a rather large and happy young guy named Ken sat down next to me. I am not a short man, but Ken made me look pretty average. You could call Ken a Gentle Giant. He became my new best friend from the start, it was pretty much love-at-first-sight with Ken. We talked after the service, and decided to go and hang out some more in the park. Ken loved hearing some of my wild and crazy stories. He seemed very upset by how I was treated at the camp. And then the Lord told me that Ken wanted to go to L.A. with me.

I said, "Hey Ken, do you want to go back to L.A. with me? The Lord just told me that you want to go, but you felt uncomfortable inviting yourself?" Ken was shocked, "Yeah . . ." he said, "Actually I was thinking, hey I should go with this guy to L.A." We were all glorifying God for His goodness and faithfulness. Ken's friend Sarah was with us and I decided that before we made any plans we should first pray. We prayed as we walked along the paths of the park. Then we remained quiet as we waited to hear from the Lord. Suddenly Sarah asked, "Robert, do you want to leave Alaska so soon?" It was the perfect question. It was the Lord! "No," I said, "Actually I was hoping to stick around for a little while before I return to L.A. I feel like I have some things I need to do here before I leave." Ken asked me if I wanted to stay with him, giving him time to submit his two-week notice, and leave with integrity. We had a plan . . . and the Lord kept me in Alaska. It was incredible. We checked me out of the hotel and I moved in with Ken.

Δ   Ω

(Again, there are so many stories I could tell about all that the Lord did while I was in Fairbanks. They are all incredible stories because the Lord was moving so miraculously. But then this book would end up being five or six hundred pages long!)

Ken had some brothers that he was excited about introducing me to. The two brothers he mentioned foremost were Rick and Gerard. Within a day or two we were at breakfast with Rick. Rick looked exactly like a Japanese monk. He was sorta' round and short with bright shining eyes and really cool, samurai hair. Rick had walked with God in a very special way that very few people ever get to experience. He started to share some of his stories with me: casting out demons, healing the sick, seeing God move like something out of the book of Acts. He told me things about the scriptures that I had never seen before. He talked about the power of God, in ways that I had only read about, but Rick had lived it. Rick became my spiritual-samurai instructor . . . my "Yoda", teaching me the deeper things of scripture. I'm sure I could have been a more moldable student, but I had seen so much bad stuff that I wasn't so quick to listen anymore, unfortunately. But in time Rick won my heart and my ear.

Rick had left everything to serve the Lord years before I had met him. He had story after story of all that the Lord had done as he was led here and there, around America. He shared some three decades of stories with Ken and me; and much wisdom God had given him throughout his life. My whole perspective of scripture was completely changing. Looking back I wish I had had more time with Rick. But being around him was what I imagine a "Spiritual Boot Camp" would be like. Rick was a little rough around the edges at times. Rick was the "Spiritual Drill Sergeant" of the boot camp.

(There are so many things about Rick that I don't feel comfortable sharing because he is such a precious brother in the Lord.) Then Rick decided to move in with us and we three became a band of brothers. Rick didn't act like our "leader" per se, but Ken and I looked up to him for guidance and spiritual wisdom. Even though Rick was obviously more experienced than we were, he never treated us like subordinates, but more like little brothers. We called him, behind his back, "The Little Big Bear" because he was short but when he slept he would snore like a huge bear. Rick was easy for me to love.

Then one day we pulled up to this coffee shop and there outside was Gerard, it seemed like he was waiting for us to show up. Ken was very excited because he had wanted me to meet Gerard for a few weeks now. Gerard was as different a man of God as any of us would ever meet. Gerard was extremely choosy with his words and often difficult to understand, but the power of God was clearly and evidently with him. Within ten minutes or so of being with Gerard, the Lord told me, "Gerard is Dan's long lost brother." I said, "What?" I will explain:

This man Dan had worked for me years ago in the mortgage business. He was an incredible salesman with an explosive and fiery personality. Dan left his mark wherever he went. No one would ever forget meeting this Dan. Here I was more than a thousand of miles from Los Angeles and the Lord told me that this Gerard was Dan's long lost brother! I didn't even know how to bring it up to him; it seemed so impossible. Over the next hour Gerard and I got to know each other so finally I asked, "Gerard do you have a brother named Dan in Southern California?"

Gerard became a little panicky and paranoid, "What did you say? How do you know this? Did my family send you here? Who are you?" As it turned out I had met Dan's long lost brother, John. John, otherwise known as Gerard, had gone through a terrible divorce some years earlier and was very hurt; hurt by the way his family reacted, hurt by what his ex-wife had done, so hurt that he just wanted to be alone for a while. So he left "the lower 48" and hid out in Fairbanks, Alaska for more than a decade. The Lord wanted me to meet him. It is, like so many of my other stories, an unimaginable pleasure to watch the Lord move. It was another genuine Jesus miracle.

Next thing you know we had this little tribe of *men of God* coming together. The other man to join us was this very mysterious Kenneth, not to be confused with Ken. Kenneth and I had actually run into each other one random day, when I was working with the camp. We had come to town for a little "R and R", and I was distraught over many of the things happening at the camp. Kenneth showed up out of nowhere and somehow he got me to tell him how sad I was. As I asked him for prayer, we literally wept together as we prayed outside of the book store where we had met. I hardly knew his name. But the Holy Spirit ministered to us while we prayed.

But then one, seemingly random day, he showed up at the church across the street from Ken's apartment. "Kenneth!" I shouted to him! He was on a bicycle and came over to greet us. Kenneth immediately became a part of our little troop too. It was so strange how he just showed up out of nowhere and came and stayed with Ken? But he was clearly to be a part of the crew. Rick and Kenneth moved into Ken's apartment with me but Gerard preferred to sleep outside. The five of us were certainly a unique band of brothers.

Δ   Ω

Throughout the rest of that summer I ministered to the Native Americans mostly. Kenneth and I got a job working for a witch, digging out her basement (which was really weird), Rick continued to teach us about the amazing things of the kingdom of God, and we hardly ever slept. Ken managed to hold his day job another couple months and the testimonies of God continued to unfold every day! It was all quite exciting! Each day was an adventure unto itself.

It was in Fairbanks that God gave me a real ministry. Looking back, before Alaska I was just learning and changing from being a businessman into a minister of the kingdom of God. Once I got together with *"the school of prophets"* in Fairbanks, my whole life changed and I was ushered into the ministry which the Lord had intended for me.

One evening we were praising God without end. It was past three in the morning but remember Alaska in the summer remains light through the night since the sun doesn't set so far north that time of year. So it was around 3:00 a.m. but still light outside, the four of us (Rick, Ken, Kenneth and I) were singing praises to God, and encouraging each other in the Lord when suddenly there was a knock at the door.

When I opened the door outside stood a taller, attractive, drunken, native girl who was looking for a cigarette and a lighter. When I saw her I exclaimed, "You aren't here for a cigarette, the Lord drew you here so that you could give your life to Jesus!" She said, "What are you guys doing here?" She was confused. She thought we were partying. I said, "We have been praying and the power of God is with us. The Lord drew you here so that you could give your life to Him!" She started to weep. She told us her whole life's story. She had walked with God when she was younger, but had since left Him and became a drunk. As we prayed for her it was like watching years of sin and depression fall off of her. She wept and praised God and glorified His holy name with us until morning. I will never ever forget that night. It was so special. I saw God's love pouring out on that girl and "us guys" were all so happy to be a part of it.

We ended up staying awake all night. Around 5:00 a.m. we went and bought breakfast food (Ken bought breakfast food for us all) and I cooked. After the power of God hit her, that native girl ended up completely sober. It was a real miracle. She said so herself. Her boyfriend came over and joined us for breakfast and he gave his life to the Lord also. We glorified God into the next day and finally our new brother and sister had to leave. We celebrated for the whole next day.

I had been ministering to these native people almost daily. One day a middle aged native woman walked up to me near the river downtown and asked me to pray for her. I said, "How do you know that I know the Lord? Why would you ask me to pray for you?" I had never seen her before. She said, "Sir, I can see Jesus in your eyes. I know you know God. Pray for me. He will hear you." As I started to pray I had a vision of her being beaten by her husband. I prayed that God would change his heart and heal their marriage. I prayed that He would set them both free of alcoholism and save them. We both wept together standing by the side of the road.

Another day there was this older man, maybe 70 years old, whom I had seen around town quite often. One day as he was walking past me on the street near the river, he said, "I know your God." But he said it with a strange tone in his voice so I responded, "Oh, so Jesus is your Lord?" He smirked, a wicked and rebellious little smirk and said, "No. I will bow to no man!" Suddenly the Holy Spirit of God fell on me and with great boldness I proclaimed to him, "Yes! You will bow! Everyone will bow! If not today, the day will come when every knee will bow and every tongue will confess that Jesus Christ is Lord!" The strangest and funniest thing happened, a demon manifested on him and he started acting like a 3- or 4-year-old child, stomping his foot on the ground saying, "No! No! I won't! I won't bow! And you can't make me!" I insisted, "But why? Why won't you? He is good. God loves you. Jesus wants to save you. He doesn't want to hurt you, He wants to love you!" But he kept stomping his foot and shouting, "I will not bow! Never! And you can't make me!" It was hilarious! I had never seen anything like it before. And I have never seen anything like it since.

It turned out that the old man was a very influential witch doctor for one of the local native tribes. And what I learned that day was that some people won't come to God not for any complex or complicated reason but simply because they are like rebellious children who don't want God, period. Sometimes it's just the devils oldest lie, 'you can be your own god'. After that the witch doctor had his eye on me. often when I was ministering to other natives around town. I will never forget him. I actually kind of liked him. I prayed for him often.

Δ   Ω

I will end my stories of Alaska with the story of a Native child named Daniel. Daniel came with the 7- and 8-year-olds to the camp when I was still working there. Daniel was a foster child and when his foster mother dropped him off she let me know what trouble I would have with him and how he often wets the bed. I assured her that everything would be fine, but certainly she knew what she was talking about.

Daniel was unruly from the start; he liked to do whatever he wanted to do. He didn't play with the other boy's and it was very difficult to communicate with him. He didn't like to talk at first. The second night he did wet the bed, all over the place and I could tell that he was very embarrassed. I did an excellent job of hiding, from the other boys that he had wet the bed and I brought him to the bathroom for him to clean himself. I think that's how I won his trust and a friendship.

After I hid the bed wetting incident Daniel realized that I was maybe an okay guy after all, and he began to warm up to me. Every day got better and better until by the fourth day he wouldn't leave my side. Daniel became my little right hand man and the most obedient of all the boys! I really started to love this kid. But we were nearing the end of the camp. We only had a few days left together.

There were only a couple days for Daniel at camp left when the whole camp went for a long hike in the woods. While we were on the hike, Daniel and William, the two boys who'd gotten especially attached to me, were right by my side while everyone else went up ahead. I started to tell them a story about God and about how God is their Father; and He would anoint them one day. I told them that being anointed is like being a knight. And I told them all about knights. These boys listened intently to every word coming out of my mouth. They were so eager to hear about knighthood.

When I was done explaining, in detail, the whole story, William said, "Mr. Robert, do you think we could be Knights one day?" (Oh how these kids can get into your heart!) I looked deeply into William's eyes and I said, "Yes William but it takes a Knight to make a Knight and you know what?" Daniel wanted in also, "What?" Both the boys asked. I said with the most serious tone I could muster, "I am a Knight of the kingdom of God!" Their eyes got very big and I could see their little hearts beating wildly. I said, "If you boys want, I could Knight you right here!" And I grabbed a long stick that looked perfectly sword-like.

The boys looked at each other and back to me, they wanted to be knighted. I made the boys both take a knee. They totally felt the gravity of the moment as they knelt down in absolute reverence and awe. I knighted them in Jesus name and I choked back tears as the Holy Spirit and the love of God dumped out on us. Being out in the woods with these precious boys as they committed their lives to Christ, as Young Knights, was one of the happiest moments of my life!

When we returned to the camp Daniel was very quiet. He grabbed my hand for the first time when we walked to go and have dinner. I purposely slowed down to enjoy the moment with him. Then just before we got close to the dining room he stopped and pulled my hand, bringing me down, closer towards him. With his big brown eyes staring into mine he asked me, "Mr. Robert, can you be my Dad?"

Wow! I was overwhelmed! What would I say? I wanted to say the perfect thing to this beautiful little boy. I didn't want to hurt him in any way and I didn't want to lie to him either. I prayed quickly and this is what came out of my mouth, "Well, we have to pray first Daniel, and ask God if I am allowed to be your dad. I would love to be your dad, but God is your Father and He chooses who He is going to allow to be your dad." I was happy to see that my answer made sense to him. He agreed and we prayed together about who would be Daniel's dad. He said

Amen when I was finished, he was clearly content and we went to go and eat.

The next day Daniel was rather unruly again. It was Saturday, around 11am his foster mom was to come and take him home. He knew full well what was about to happen and he was having a very difficult time with it. I was too, quite frankly. I didn't want to see him go. Truth be told, I would have adopted him if I could have. He wouldn't listen to me all that morning and when we went to chapel it was my turn to preach to all the kids of the camp, but Daniel wouldn't come inside. When I was finished I went looking for him. He was outside playing in the dirt with some bugs. I could see the sadness dripping off of his face. I was sad too.

I said, "God is going to take care of you Daniel. But I don't want you to go either," a few tears ran down my face. He was surprised to see me weeping and he reached up and wiped a tear from my eye. Then he said, "It will be okay." I was surprised how he started to comfort me. It was cute. Maybe he just needed to see someone crying over him. Maybe no one ever had cried for Daniel before. When his foster mom came he was back to his happy self. She grabbed his things and started to take him towards the car. I waved goodbye as they walked down the driveway towards the car. When Daniel got to the car he stopped, turned back around, ran to me and jumped into my arms; he held on to me and hugged my neck really tight. It was a perfect goodbye. I'll never forget it as long as I live.

Later on I learned that no one had ever seen Daniel hug anyone before. His mom told the leaders of the camp that I had changed Daniel's life. Truth is that that little boy changed my life.

Months later, after all the drama of my leaving the camp, meeting Ken and the prophets, and just before Ken and I left Fairbanks for Los Angeles together in his new car, I was preaching and sharing stories outside near the river with a group of natives. They loved to hear me talk about my adventures with God. Herman was there. He was the tribal elder whom I had befriended and found favor with earlier that summer. (Herman is a whole other chapter of a book!) There were maybe ten other people from Herman's tribe listening to me telling stories.

Somehow I started telling the story of Daniel, and this woman suddenly burst into tears. She practically ran away from me and almost all of the natives left to go and console her. I tried to go over to her to find out what I had done wrong, but Herman would not allow it. I said, "What did I do Herman?" He was angry with me and Herman had never been angry with me; in fact he bought me breakfast many times and offered to purchase my flight home to L.A. Herman and I had become close friends. *What had happened?* I wondered.

Herman went to go and talk with her and when he returned he said, "Who are you?" I said, "What? What are you talking about Herman? You know me. I'm Robert, the traveling minister guy." He said, "Who are you really? Do you work for the state or something?' I said, "What are you talking about?" It turned out that Daniel was that crying woman's son. He had been taken away from her some eighteen months earlier and she hadn't heard anything about him in all that time. She lived in a village far from Fairbanks and just so happened to run into me; and I *just so happened* to be sharing that story about Daniel when she was standing there with her tribe listening to my story. It was another genuine Jesus miracle.

I tried to console them and tell them all that God had done this miracle to comfort her and to at least let her know that He was taking care of her son. But the pain of losing Daniel was just too great, so no one wanted to talk to me anymore. I understood and left them alone. I prayed that the Lord would comfort Daniel's mom. I prayed for Daniel often that summer. There was nothing else I could do.

It was time for Ken and I to head for Los Angeles. Summer was over. Soon the snow would come and we wouldn't be able to drive thru Canada once the weather turned cold. It was mid-September. Rick wouldn't let us leave without first baptizing me again. He baptized me in the tub in Ken's bathroom. It was really funny and the Lord did something in me that day to restore some innocence. We left Rick, Gerard, Kenneth and all our other friends with great sorrow.

And then we headed south...

Chapter 8

We experienced the hand of God all the way down to California. We met and ministered to many people along the way. Ken's new car kept breaking down on the way thru Canada, but that was giving us more chances to minister as we traveled south. It was definitely the Lord because the car would only break down when we got to a town; and then it would miraculously fix itself. This happened at least four times as we drove thru Canada and on down through Idaho to Seattle. By the time we got to Seattle the car had completely fixed itself and we never had a problem with it again. Literally. No mechanic was ever able to find anything wrong with the car, but somehow it kept not starting. Then for no reason that anyone could find, it just fixed itself. It was clear to us that God wanted us ministering our way thru Canada.

It took us almost a week to make it to Seattle. Then we were back with some of my family for a short while in California, and onward to Los Angeles. We ended up staying at a house full of up-and-coming ministers. There were eleven or twelve of us men on that property, ranging in age from 20-years-old up to 50-something (I'm not sure of Rodney's age?) That was a tremendous season for Ken and I to be with other brothers!

Let me tell you, Iron sharpened a lot of Iron while we stayed in that place. Looking back I can't count how many ministries were started by the men who were living in that home at that time. It was a very difficult, pride-swallowing season, but very fruitful; very refining. Ken and I went onward to Arizona, and shortly after that he felt led to go back to Alaska. But we would have one more grand adventure together before Ken left me.

We decided to drive to Phoenix in the evening because it was so hot in the daytime. It was 2 or 3 in the morning and we were in the middle of the desert. Ken still smoked from time to time then so he wanted to have a smoke break. We both wanted to see the stars without light interference, (the stars are incredible in the middle of the desert at night) so we found a very dark place in the middle of nowhere, half-way to Phoenix, and pulled off the freeway.

About a block or so off I-10 we came upon a newer Mercedes Benz broken down, with a man sitting inside, obviously upset. Ken jumped into savior mode, but I was unusually quite cautious. Ken wanted to check it out. I said I would wait in the car and keep the engine running to make sure that nothing happened. Then out of the Mercedes pops this little man in his late 50's completely drunk and upset. Ken was very safe. Ken was probably double (or triple) the size of this little guy. I parked the car ahead of the Mercedes and got out to investigate.

The man was beyond drunk. With the few mechanical skills Ken and I could muster we managed to figure out that he had put oil in his car but was so drunk that he left the oil cap off and so all oil from the engine had splattered out; he was driving the car from L.A. without oil when finally, the engine seized. It was a little humorous actually; this little drunk man, with the thick Russian accent, out in the middle of nowhere, with his blown up car.

There would be no quick fix in getting his car up and running. We asked Alex where he was headed and it turned out that his destination was only a couple hours out of the way from where we were going. Ken and I decided that we should take him

Alex started to tell us his whole life's story in the car. The man had been a criminal for most of his life: heavily involved with illegal activities throughout Southern California. We didn't want to know so many details, but he just kept talking. He showed us pictures of all kinds of famous people, with several politicians at their criminal parties. It was a little frightening actually, being with a professional (or ex-professional) criminal.

I had to really fight the fear that was trying to jump on me. As his story continued it got better and better and my fear began to subside.

It turned out that somehow he had quit being a criminal. Through some sorta' loop hole they let him out. He was going to Arizona to marry this girl and start a new life with her. He told us some amazing things about HOW HE FOUND JESUS! He told us about a time when satan appeared to him in his apartment and he knew he had to give his life over to Jesus or else the devil would kill him. These stories were even hard for me to believe even after all I had already lived with the Lord. (Remember how randomly we met this guy in the middle of nowhere in the desert!)

As he was telling his stories he kept saying to us, "I know you guys aren't allowed to tell me who you are . . . " and then he would laugh and continue telling us about his life. He didn't really stop talking the whole three or four hour drive to his fiancés house. It was very hard for me to believe all this. I mean we accidentally got off the freeway at that exit and there he was!? Unbelievable stuff, especially considering this whopper of a story he was telling us now. But on and on he went.

He wanted to drink again because he was starting to sober up. None of us had slept all night and now the sun was up. I was not in any mood to have him drink more, but Ken had so much more compassion then me. I'm glad I listened to Ken and let him drink. I watched him down a whole bottle of liquor in seconds flat. And then within a few minutes he was completely drunk again. The Lord showed up in the midst of all this and explained to me, "Robert, the man is very afraid. He is afraid that he is hoping for something that is going to fall apart. He genuinely wants to start a new life with this woman and he isn't convinced that she is going to love him and accept him." Once the Lord explained the situation better to me, my attitude changed immediately. Then I had compassion for him, like Ken.

I started to encourage him, telling him that his new life would be wonderful and God was going to do everything for him; even set him free of his alcohol addiction. I really felt the presence of God talking to him about these things; we all did. He started weeping when I was encouraging him. He said, "Look, I know who you guys are. You don't have to tell me. I can't believe He sent you both to me! Who am I?" And he continued to talk this way for quite a while. I still didn't know what he was talking about.

When we finally got to his fiancés house I was overjoyed to see that he wasn't lying, at all. Every single thing he'd said, she confirmed over breakfast without him prompting her. It was very clear: God had done *a great Miracle for this older ex-criminal.* We prayed for them and commanded that the alcohol addiction be broken off of his life in Jesus name. He agreed and promised never to drink again. A wonderful peace came over me, because I really felt like somehow these two were going to make a life together. I just knew it was all going to work out. Ken and I drove away in tears again; so happy to have been used by the hand of God to love one of His children.

Maybe a year later they contacted me to tell me how they had been. His fiancé, who was now his wife, explained to me that Alex had never believed we were real people. He completely and totally thought that we were angels sent from God to save him. *And that's not the last time someone thought Ken was an angel.* As the story goes, he never drank again. He started a painting business; they go to church every Sunday and Praise God for their new life. God is so good. He is awesome! I love Him so much!

Δ Ω

I want to tell you a couple of sad stories now:

When I was living in Oregon, I was put in a very uncomfortable position with a certain pastor. He had been diagnosing many children and youths has having "ADD" or "ADHD" or "Bipolar" to their parents, and the parents were so affected by his diagnosis they were having these kids put on very powerful drugs. It was a real mess. I tried to talk to him about it several times, but he wouldn't listen.

On one occasion we got into a big argument about it and I got angry, I said, "You have to stop doing this. You are a pastor, not a psychiatrist or a physician. You are a minister of the kingdom of God, you pray for healing and restoration and the power of God to help these kids and their families! That is your job. That is who you are." He continued to argue and attack me. Finally, I said, "If you don't believe me now, you will believe me when you have a heart attack because God is going to judge you and He will get your attention because you won't listen."

I hated saying these things to him because in truth he was one of the good guys. He wasn't some hypocritical, arrogant pastor; he was really trying to help and in the trenches every day, he wasn't rich or high and mighty, and ruling the church. He was in so many ways a real pastor. But this was a big problem in his ministry and God wanted me to talk with him about it.

After I warned him about the heart attack he got very quiet and we ended the conversation. I should mention here that I believe with all my heart that God was trying to get this man back to Himself. But he could not see what God was doing. It was very sad and I prayed for him often after I left Oregon. I left Oregon shortly after that confrontation.

Eight or nine months later he called me and said, "I guess you heard the news?" I hadn't. He told me about how he had had a heart attack some three months after we had that argument and he was having a year-long sabbatical, praying about his life, seeking God all over again. My heart broke as he told me these things. I wasn't in the least bit happy to hear the news. As he was confessing his sins over the phone I stopped him and I said, "You are my elder in the Lord. I wish I hadn't had to say those things to you. You are a mighty man of God and God is going to work even greater things thru your life. Please don't talk to me about these things ever again. You are a hero of the faith to me and many others. How many people have you served over the years?" He was very humbled and wouldn't really take the exhortation very well. But I believe he was edified.

That lovely man went on to rebuild his incredible ministry for homeless youth. He and his team have affected countless lives and he has been healthy ever since. I am happy to say we are still friends to this day.

Another sad story similar to the one I just told comes from California some years after I left Oregon. A pastor much like the one in Oregon, ironically, also running homeless centers and street outreaches came into my life. He was a soldier for the Lord no doubt but he had clearly gotten lost into the *prosperity gospel* or what I call *the false prosperity gospel*. He was living two lives and commingling them. He was creating business to fund his ministry but they were so intertwined together that there was no telling where the business ended and the ministry began. But there was more.

I saw something like a vision where the Lord showed me the wicked spirits that had gotten attached to him somewhere along the way. He needed to stop. He needed to rest and get healthy again. He needed to start over. I started to pray for him. I was around him and his ministry for four or five before finally things started to come to a head. I had to say something. I started fasting and praying for him and what the Lord wanted me to say.

It must have been five or six days into the fast that the Lord gave me His Word. I delivered the Word with great humility and compassion to that minister of God but I was completely rejected, even laughed at. I said, "Pastor, I have only respect for you and all the things that you have done for the Lord and I have sought the Lord diligently on your behalf, and this is what the Lord said. You have to stop doing both business and ministry. Chose one or the other and you have to take a break in the process to get healthy again. God wants you to take a sabbatical." It was a longer word than what I am writing now. But the point is, he rejected it completely.

I strongly warned him, "If you do not change judgment is coming to your life. I see very bad judgment." He was obviously uncomfortable listening to me, but he was also very puffed up with pride. I hated being in that position, but I was there to serve the Lord and try to help this man, this pastor. With much sorrow our meeting ended, and I left California shortly thereafter.

A short while after I left him, they found a brain tumor something like 15 percent of the size of his brain. As the story goes, his life plummeted downhill. It was such a sad story. None of this was God's will. God had a plan in place to save him. But he wasn't open or humble to the word of God. God did many things to show him back then, that I hear from God, but he wasn't interested, not in the least bit. It was very very sad. This is *not in any way* God's will for the Body of Christ.

△   Ω

Back to Arizona with Ken; we had lost the place where we were staying. We were somewhat stranded and sleeping in a friend's office when Ken went back to Alaska. I guess I was alone only a day or two when this man Gary came in and started to talk business with me. I told him some about my life and all of a sudden I started to smell something like wet dog. The smell grew so strong that it was almost bothering me. Just then the Lord said, "Gary has a dog that he loves. Ask him about his dog." I interrupted him mid-sentence and said, "Do you have a dog that you love?" And Gary's whole face lit up! "Who? Chezzy!" He exclaimed!

Anyone who knows Gary knows that Gary loves his 'Chezzy'. He said, "You want to go and meet her?" Within minutes we were in his car and headed to his house. (Let me remind you here that Gary did not know that I was without a place to stay and sleeping in my friend's office for nearly a week.) We got to his house and Val, his wife, was there. I will never forget meeting those two.

I couldn't have been there more than three or four minutes when Val said, "Hey, where are you staying? Do you need a place?" I said, "What?" She said, "Yeah. If you need a place to stay we have an extra room." I couldn't believe it. God had provided. It was amazing! And these lovely people became my new best friends. Gary was at times an uncle, other times a brother, but he has always been my good friend. God has brought Gary and I through many many adventures together over the years. I love him very much.

Over the next couple years, I went back and forth from Arizona to California over and again. God was always very clear about when to go and when to leave. I was with Gary and another longtime friend named Charley a lot those years. (I would need to write another book to share about my friend Charley. He had a huge impact on me in my early twenties. We were very close friends then.)

I met Charley back when I was in business. He was a believer and like me he was offended by organized religion. He had a saying that he loved to repeat, "Religion is satan's trump card." We couldn't have come from more different backgrounds. Charley's father was very famous cancer doctor in the 60's and 70's who was put in jail in California for curing cancer with vitamins. It's a long story about all that happened to Charley's dad and their family; a very long and tragic story. Like I said, I could easily write a whole book about Charley and our time together.

So Gary and Charley were my Arizona buddies, when I was in L.A. I resided in the young ministers-discipleship house and then there was my friend Frank in Central California. Frank was a brother from day one, a big brother, but a brother none the less. God worked mightily in our friendship to bond us in the Spirit. We were changed a lot by the hand of God while Frank and I were together. Gary, Charley and Frank—it's hard to come by men like this. I was blessed.

This was a tremendous season of refinement and preparation in my life. But preparation for what? I could tell God was doing something in me but I couldn't see what it was or where He was taking me. Talk about walking by faith!

Now that the characters are in place I can tell you more of the story ...

Chapter 9

I was staying at Frank's office for a little while, and the Lord was really teaching me nightly about intercession. I sometimes would be awake three or four hours a night praying and talking with the Lord about it. He was explaining to me many things about the way His kingdom works; Jesus being the absolute model of intercession.

A couple months before I was at Frank's place I had gone up into the mountains alone, to fast and pray; I wanted to seek God for some answers, and really come to walk with Him like Rick, in Alaska, had shared with me. I fasted and prayed for days on end and waited to hear God's voice. Just then, as Forrest Gump liked to say, "God showed up."

I was taken in a dream or vision out of my body early in the morning around 4:00 a.m. I saw myself leaving my body behind in the room. I was flown over the city of Los Angeles. I saw the whole downtown destroyed. It looked like a bomb had gone off. The high rise buildings were burning, and everywhere L.A. was afire. Many of the buildings had collapsed and the whole place was in ruins. Then almost as suddenly as I was taken out of my body, I was brought back into the room. My heart raced and I asked the Lord what had happened to L.A. It was as if the Lord Himself was in the room, I heard Him so clearly; He said, "I am going to destroy L.A. with an earthquake."

I don't know what you would ask the Lord having had such an experience, but what I wanted to know was, "Why are you telling this to *me*!" The Lord said, "I want you to intercede for the city." I responded, "Who am I to pray for a whole city?" The Lord didn't respond.

I was then at Frank's office a month or so later learning to be an intercessor.

Δ Ω

I think what surprised me the most that the Lord would use me to intercede was that I was still so sinful. While I wasn't partying and drinking like I used to, I still had girlfriends along the way. I do not like to admit this fact, except that it is important to mention, if I am going to paint an accurate picture of God's working with me all these years. I don't want anyone to think that I had arrived at the pinnacle of holiness when the Lord started His calling in my life. But I did come to hate the fact that I was so sinful. I prayed about it often.

I think this was why it was so easy for my friends and family to doubt that I was being used by God; they would see me in all these short term and broken relationships, and say to themselves, "What man of God could possibly be bouncing around America from girlfriend to girlfriend." And, "Why would God listen to such a man?" I agreed with them on multiple occasions, even trying to bargain with the Lord, saying, "Surely you must have someone better suited for this job than me."

But the Lord seemed to be convinced that I was the right guy. He would assure me on occasion, "My grace is sufficient for you." He would show me the brokenness of others of His servants, and comfort me. God is very very different than I was raised to believe. He determines who will be His servants. We do not determine who God will choose. And, *yes*, He uses broken vessels.

The churches we grew up in, and the general culture of the religious world, most everything is based on judgment; *incorrect/ bad judgment*. God is only a judge at the very end. The rest of the time we are judging our own selves (I can show you scripture on this another time). God is our Father. He loves us. He is very different than we have been taught. Trust me. If you knew just how messed up I have been while the Lord was doing amazing things through me, you would know God isn't anything like we have been taught!

I am in no way writing and giving anyone an excuse to sin. Sin still leads to death. We still do not want to sin. But the scripture still says, "Blessed is the man in whom the Lord does not impute sin." And again, "Blessed is the man in whom the Lord imputes righteousness." Again still, "There is none righteous, no not one." So that's enough trying to use our brokenness as an excuse for not loving the world and telling people about Jesus. "We are saved through faith by grace." Amen.

Here is a good story for you, illustrating my point:

One time I was in a bar with some friends from my past business days. In fact, I was with Jeff, another friend. I might as well mention here, since he has a lot to do with the "intercessor" story I am starting to tell, Jeff was raised in a very religious household, but grew up and rejected it all, basically because it made him angry that his mom told him that Jesus *told her* to divorce his dad. (I don't know if he ever forgave his mom or God for that.) So Jeff had taken me out to this bar to celebrate something, we were eating and drinking, I was sipping wine and had had two glasses.

Jeff has long been a friend of mine. I had long hoped he would find the Lord. At the bar, somehow I started to talk with the bartender about Jesus and the people next to me got involved in the conversation, several more joined until seven or eight people at the bar were listening to me preach; "Religion hasn't the power to save you, we are saved in Jesus name!" It was a wonderful time. The joy of the Lord was with us in the middle of that bar. I have had many such experiences over the years ministering God's grace.

Through these many experiences I have come to learn that God is very different than we think. God loves us. He isn't trying to harm us. He wants to teach us and help us to be blessed; and no longer live under the curse. He is always pursuing us, doing everything He can to win our affection and trust. God is the perfect Father, always. He is holy. In Him we are made "the righteousness of Christ". He displays His mercy and His grace thru or lives. And that is why He would use a broken vessel like me to become one of His sons.

Jesus will get all the glory out of my life! Amen.

Δ   Ω

During these six to eight months, I was going back and forth between California and Arizona. God continued to speak on one main topic, "Interceding on behalf of others". He changed my mind about many many conclusions I had come to. God wants MERCY and not judgment. It is TRUE, God is in fact Good!

One unexpected night, maybe 1 in the morning while at Frank's office, the Lord woke me. I awoke to this very real and tangible fear for L.A. I thought, *maybe its tonight! Maybe the earthquake is going to destroy L.A. tonight!* Well Brian, my dear younger brother lived in L.A. then, and thinking about him being hurt or killed in an earthquake was more than enough to get me moving. Also my beloved Aunt Lori and Uncle Dennis lived there, so I had to try to do something. Suddenly my mind raced to the story of Lot and how, as long as he was in Sodom, God would not destroy the city. So I hopped in my car (actually Ken's car, he had loaned it to me) and headed south.

It was about 2 am or so and I was praying as I drove the three hours south, "Father hold on! I am hurrying! Have mercy Father! Wait!" The closer to the city I got, the more nervous I became, hoping that I was, in fact, a Lot-type character before the Lord. I didn't stop praying the whole 3-hour drive. I had no real direction from the Lord as to where I should go, so I thought of a park where I like to pray often outside of the city. And I headed there.

It was 5:00 a.m. or so when I got to a coffee shop. I got my coffee and headed to the park to pray and listen to the Lord. As I walked around the park the Lord started to give very detailed instructions about what to do. He told me to go and pray with three very specific people: this pastor I had known for years but had lost touch with, my brother, and Jeff my old time business friend. I repeated back to the Lord, "You want me to tell them about the earthquake and pray with them?" The Lord was very clear, "Yes."

Well, this is going to be interesting, I thought. My brother hadn't been walking with the Lord in years and Jeff wanted nothing to do with God. At that time Jeff was also upset with the Lord for what he called, "killing his brother, Scott." (It's a long story about what happened with Jeff's brother...very tragic. Jeff often spoke about this.) This pastor had known me since I was 13 or so, and would in no way find me anything like a prophet of God. (Mark 6:4) But I obeyed the voice of God nonetheless.

I got to the pastor's house first, being that he lived very close to the park. He was home. I was invited in and I started to explain all that the Lord had told me, beginning from fasting on top of the mountain onward to being at Frank's office and coming to L.A. that morning. The pastor's wife spoke for him, saying, "Robert, you are not an old testament prophet. God does not speak to people like this anymore. You need to consider getting some real help. We do not believe anything that you are saying." I was shocked and angry, hearing her say this. I tried my best to control my emotions.

I asked the pastor if his wife spoke for him. He looked afraid . . . I was calling him out. He looked towards his wife and she sorta' nodded as if to say, "You know what to do." And he looked back at me and said, "Well, yes." I was astonished! He started to back track a little, maybe realizing how difficult a situation this was. Let me say that I do know he cared/cares about me. But he wasn't able to confront the situation any differently. He absolutely wasn't able to stand up to his wife. At the end of the conversation he said, "I just don't believe that this is the Lord." So I left their house immediately.

I called my brother next. He interrupted me half way thru my story and said, "Are you really telling me that you think God told you that there would be an earthquake today?" I said, "Yes." And he said, "Robert, I'm at work. Don't worry, Robert. There isn't going to be an earthquake today. Everything will be just fine. Don't call me anymore while I am at work about stuff like this." He hung up the phone on me. My precious brother Brian, the very logical and organized Brian, this was surely a lot for him to handle. But the Lord did tell me to bring him in on it and to pray with him, so I had to obey.

Finally, it was time for "the big unbeliever" Jeff. Around 4:00 p.m. or so, Jeff took me to a pool hall and ordered plenty of beer, wine and snacks while we talked. He knew I was about to drop something pretty heavy on him by the things I mentioned in the brief conversation we had had on the phone so Jeff brought along a companion to help him navigate through "Robert", and all that I would bring with me. Jeff and his helper, Taylor (who was actually my friend from high school) listened as I told them the long testimony about the earthquake coming to L.A. at any moment. Putting myself in their shoes they actually did a pretty darn good job listening to the whole story from start to finish.

Finally, Jeff responded, he said, "Robert, if anyone else in the whole world ever came to me and told me that God told them that there was an earthquake coming to L.A. I would laugh at them and probably never talk to them again but because it's you, I am listening. What do you think the Lord wants us to do?" I couldn't believe it. Jeff, "The non-Believer", the money-loving, business guy, who was upset with God, actually turned out to be the one with faith. I never would have guessed it.

A short hour later we were back at Jeff's posh L.A. pad and on our knees praying that the Lord would have mercy and spare the city! We couldn't have prayed for more than 5 or 10 minutes when this incredible feeling of peace came over my whole body and I knew that the Lord had heard us! We prayed, I said, "Amen." and Jeff agreed, saying, "Amen." And just like that it was all over.

Jeff got up from off of his knees and said, "That's it?" I said, "Yep, that's it. Our job is done." Jeff said, "Wow. That sure was easy. How do you know that the Lord heard us?" I said, "I feel peace for the first time since 2:00 a.m. this morning. I am totally sure that He heard us." And Jeff seemed content. He told me to stay the night and drive home in the morning. I was so tired I agreed.

The next day about 11am I was half way back to Frank's office just north of L.A., when a 6.1 earthquake hit a few miles away from downtown! Jeff was the first one to call me. Brian texted shortly after that, and many others contacted me to say, "We cannot believe that God told you there would be an earthquake today!" But God hadn't really told me about that earthquake. I was a little confused, I have to admit, but I decided that there was maybe going to be a really huge earthquake, but since Jeff and I prayed, the Lord had mercy on the city.

Jeff called me later that day and agreed. He said, "I figure that God spared the city. Maybe that earthquake was going to be over 8.0, but because we prayed it was just 6.1." It was unbelievable. I *did in fact* hear from God! I would love to say that I knew for certain that I was hearing from Him all along, but that isn't exactly how faith works ...

God was teaching me to trust Him. He was showing me that He *is in fact* with me.

And I do have to say that it sure was nice to know that I wasn't crazy after all.

Chapter 10

In hindsight, Frank's office was a place of great breakthrough for me. I was diligently seeking the Lord about publishing the book and if that was not His plan, I was praying about what would be my next step. In those days I was keeping a website with all kinds of my writings, entitled, "Jesus did not start a Religion—Journey to the kingdom of God".

To this day I am not sure how he found my website, but a pastor from Uganda had stumbled upon it, and kept in touch with me some six months. He had never asked for money or done anything alarming; he seemed to simply want to communicate, harmless enough. One morning I awoke at Frank's office to a rather unexpectedly long email from him, his name is Unity. In the email he explained that a woman in his church had a vision of me coming to Uganda and preaching at their place. The email was two or more pages long, filled with details about my life and things he would have no way of knowing from just reading those articles.

I have faith but I didn't have enough faith to jump on a flight just from having read his email, so I responded, "If this is what the Lord truly is asking of me please pray that He will confirm this word. And as soon as He opens the door I will be on a flight to Africa." It was about 7:30 in the morning when I sent that email to Uganda.

About 8:00 a.m. I arrived at the quaint little café where I often started my day. It was just a few blocks from the beach. I really enjoyed my mornings there. The cafe was unusually empty when I arrived. I sat down at a table, one as removed as I could find. I did not want to be disturbed while I read my bible and wrote in my prayer journal. And wouldn't you know it? The only customers to show up at the café that morning decided to sit awkwardly close to me. I remember being irritated as the young woman and her boy friend sat down next to me.

Like something from a dream, the young woman started pulling Ugandan money out of her purse and exclaiming joyfully to her boyfriend, "Honey, look at the money from Uganda, isn't it beautiful?" I had to really get hold of myself, because I thought this was some kind of conspiracy. I had only received that email 30 minutes ago from Uganda! And now this incredibly white, suburban-looking girl was remarking about their currency. What was going on here? I couldn't help but feel flustered.

Finally, as I listened to her carrying on for another ten or fifteen minutes about Uganda I had to interrupt. I said, "Excuse me, did you just return from Uganda?" She said, "Yeah, I flew into LAX last night and I was so jet lagged that I couldn't sleep. So we got up and came here for a coffee." I explained my reason for intruding on their conversation and showed them the email I had just received from Unity, moments earlier. She was astonished also. She jumped up and said, "This is a real miracle! Honey, can you believe it? You *are* going to Uganda, Robert! God is really sending you to Africa?"

As we talked I found out that neither she nor her boyfriend believed in God. Yet still she proclaimed, "God is sending you to Uganda!" Suddenly I had my answer about what I would be doing with God next, He was sending me to Africa.

I told Frank all that had happened and we started to pray about when and how I would get there.

Δ   Ω

Remember how I told you about my dad, Roger, technically my step dad, and how he wanted to fight me and then disappeared with no one seeing him for seven years? Well, dad was about to show up again.

As I prayed it became clear that I wasn't leaving right away for Africa. Yet God continued to confirm His word that He was sending me. I had gone to Los Angeles to visit the minister's discipleship house and do a few things God had put on my heart. I had received two prophetic words that God was going to equip me, and then send me to Africa. I got several prophetic words; they were all basically the same message, *Wait on the Lord.*

One day I was writing an email to Gary, in Arizona, to tell him the whole story when God confirmed the whole trip again. I was in the process of writing the line, "God is sending me to Africa ..." when the door burst open and an African man walked right into the room! I have never seen an African man in that house before, so I was shocked, being that I had only just written the letters of Africa, "Afri . . ." in the email! I blurted out, "What country in Africa are you from?"

He was kinda offended and responded in a thick Kenyan accent, "Just because I am black doesn't mean I am from Africa." I said, "Don't be offended man. God just did a miracle! Look at what I was just writing!" And I explained the whole story. As I did the Holy Ghost came upon us both and he started to prophesy over me in the thickest Kenyan accent, "My dear brother, God is sending you to Africa! And you are going to do great signs and wonders! You are going to reveal His glory and His works will follow you wherever you go! God is with you dear brother!" I wept as the Spirit confirmed every single one of his words. It was a wonderful time, receiving such encouragement from my Father.

The *road* can be long with the Lord at times. What I mean is living by faith has lots of ups and downs, because all along the way we are learning to trust our Father who isn't always so easy to see. Sometimes He conceals Himself and His ways. His ways are truly beyond finding out. This season, waiting to leave the country, became just that for me, a very long, difficult time, *waiting upon Him.* Then in the midst of all this waiting, my dad showed up.

He called Brian to tell him that he had just been diagnosed with stage-four (basically terminal) cancer, and he wanted to make amends with us before departing. Wow! This was all a lot to handle. At least now it made a lot of sense why the Lord was slowing me down from leaving. It was so sad. My dad, whom I hadn't been very close to for years now, was dying. And clearly not expected to live ...

He told Brian, "Tell Robert that if we get together I want him to promise not to pray for me to get healed and not to talk with me about natural health cancer cures." Brian repeated the message word for word. It made me even more sad hearing that dad was completely giving up. I don't want to tell every detail of what happened with my dad. I love him too much. And it's very personal to write in this way. I never did talk with him face to face before he died. My heart was breaking.

I was in Arizona when the Lord said to me about 10:00 p.m., unless you go to Los Angeles now you will never see your dad alive again. I listened to the Lord, got in my (Ken's) car and drove to L.A. I got to the hospice center about 4:30 a.m. and went in to see him.

I will never forget how horrible he looked, my poor dad, he looked like the pictures you see of the concentration camp survivors from WWII, like bones dipped in skin. He was a good man, my dad, no one is perfect, but he never ever called me his stepson, he never treated me any differently than his own daughters (my half sisters) and he loved us with everything he had to give. The divorce ruined him. He never got over my mom. He loved her. It was so hard to look at him. I was so sad.

I still remember us sitting on the balcony of his condo a year or so after the divorce when I was just starting to make money. I guess I was 21 years old. We both smoked then, so we would smoke a pack of cigarettes and discuss how he was going to get my mom back. We would smoke and drink wine sometimes until midnight. I would try to encourage him about how he could win her back and he would tell me why I was naïve. But he still listened to every thought I had. He had made some big mistakes, sure, but I saw it in his eyes, he still loved my mom, and I just wanted to try to help them figure it out and get back together. It was a very sad time of life for me, for him, for my whole family ...

All these memories and more ran through my mind as I sat next to him in the hospice center. Finally I said to him, "What happened to you, dad?" I tried to touch him, but it was hard, he looked so strange. Then the Lord said, "You can touch his hands. His hands look the same as before." And sure enough his hands had oddly lost no weight like the rest of his body. So I held on to his hands and talked with him. He was so deep in a coma he didn't respond to a word I said. But I kept talking anyway.

I knelt at his bedside and prayed, "Father it says in Your Word that we have the power in Jesus name to forgive sins and so I am asking you now in Jesus mighty name to forgive all my dad's sins. Throw them as far as the east is from the west and remember them no more. Welcome him into your kingdom with loving and open arms Father. In Jesus name I pray. Amen." I couldn't get up off the ground. I sat there next to him holding his hand, wondering what it is like to die.

I went to my brother's house about 8:00 a.m. and drank some coffee with him and his lovely wife, "Julia-Gulia". Brian and I went back to the hospital about 10:30 that morning and we talked with dad together. I asked him, "What do you think, Brian? Should we pray that God sends an angel to take dad home? He doesn't want to live anymore and I'm sure he is in a lot of pain." Brian agreed that Jesus would hear us. I prayed, "Father send an angel to take my dad home ..." As we prayed dad's new wife and her kids all walked into the room. Brian and I were weeping as they walked in.

Dad's new wife started sobbing very loudly upon seeing us and we thought it best to give her some time alone with him. My dad died around noon. The Lord sent him an angel just as we had asked and he was in heaven with Jesus, seeing things so much more clearly. He could have peace now. The horribly tragic ending to my dad's life was finally over.

My sister Rebekah, Roger's first born had showed up at the hospital. She was weeping very hard, knowing that dad had passed away. Praise God my dad was able to make amends with my sisters and Brian and leave this fallen world with some closure. He I am certain he knows much better now and he prays for us every day, literally interceding before the throne of God. We will be with him again one day so it's not as sad as it could have been.

("It must be awesome being able to pray for us kids, dad. We will see you soon enough. Love you forever!")

Δ   Ω

We did a weekend funeral of sorts for dad. We weren't really able to do a formal funeral so Brian, Rebekah, Samantha, and I just hung out all weekend, looking through old pictures and driving around L.A. to some of his favorite places. We shared stories about dad and laughed about his unique sense of humor. It was a very intimate and special time with my brother and sisters. I hadn't felt so close to Rebekah in years. Samantha was the most vulnerable I had ever seen her before. Dad gave those girls a gift before he died. I saw it. It really worked dad!

After the weekend was over I knew that it was time to leave L.A. for Uganda. I had unfinished business in Arizona, so that Monday I headed back to Scottsdale. Ken was meeting me there to get his car back and then the plan was that he would return to Alaska while I would leave the country for Africa.

It was overwhelming in a bad way, how I ended up leaving the U.S.

Chapter 11

Before I left the country and before my dad died, I fasted and prayed for one week while at the minister's discipleship house in L.A. Even though dad told me not to pray for him, I just had to try. I fasted and prayed and God responded, three different people told me that my dad didn't want to live anymore, and that God wouldn't heal him because he was praying to die. It was at least an answer, even if it wasn't what I wanted to hear.

But while I was fasting, my friend Rodney at the discipleship house invited me to attend "an invite only" prayer meeting that was, at that time, being held at the birthplace of the Azusa Street Revival. When we pulled up to the Bonnie Brae house, Rodney explained the whole story to me. I had known very little of the history of the Azusa Street Revival Rodney was sharing. As he shared, the Holy Spirit came upon me, and I just knew something incredible was about to happen.

We were early to the meeting, so when the leader of the prayer group showed up we were waiting in the parking lot. Rodney and I walked with him to the front door of the house. His name was Thomas. Almost immediately he started prophesying over me. Thomas said, "You are intelligent and that is good but tonight you are going to have to turn your brain off a little bit. You won't be able to figure out what is going on. You are going to have to trust the Lord. He is going to do something very big in your life tonight." Now I was more excited than ever, but honestly, I was still thinking that Thomas was prophesying about healing my dad.

When Thomas' right hand man, Richard, showed up they both decided to pray for me. I felt like I was in a *Lord of the*

Rings movie. Thomas fit the description of the king, Legolas and Richard was the spitting image of the dwarf, Gimli (except a little taller). It was surreal being there with them, and it got stranger by the minute.

As they prayed for me, they had to hold me up because the Holy Ghost was falling on me with such heaviness, it was hard to stand. When they were through I looked up and there above Thomas' head were three glowing orbs, one was white and one was yellow and the other light-orange. I looked at Thomas and said, "There are three glowing balls above your head." He said, rather nonchalantly, "Yeah. Those are angels. God is going to do something incredible in your life tonight!"

As the other people arrived, and the night began, something like wind kept moving past me, like in a circular pattern. I couldn't feel it so much physically, but something kept trying to push me around in a circle. It's hard to explain. Thomas had sort of collapsed onto his knees. He was shaking and convulsing as the Holy Ghost fell on him with great power! As the Holy Spirit increased in the room, one woman started to travail, like giving birth and the Lord told me, "She is interceding for you." I said, "Why?" The Lord said, "Trust me."

I was trying to figure out what was going on as this wind-feeling kept pulling on me, turning me to my right, but I was fighting it. No one could have known what was going on because I was fighting this feeling. But just then, Thomas, still shaking, yelled out, "Robert, don't flight Him just go along with it!" I thought "How could he have known that I was fighting this feeling?" So I decided to surrender to whatever it was that the Lord was doing with me.

I allowed that wind sensation to pull me around and then I fell on the ground "as a dead man"! Immediately I was taken into a vision. I saw the Archangel Michael walking towards me with a huge sword in his hand. The sword was so big that he couldn't lift it so he was dragging it behind him. Michael was beautiful! His face looked almost feminine he was so beautiful, but he was very well built, and wearing some serious silver battle armor. He was glorious to look at, and intimidating to be sure.

As Michael came near to me, he picked up that sword with all his might and plunged it into my chest! As he did, I felt a very real heat in my chest as I lay on the floor in the Bonnie Brae house. Then I saw a serpent with fiery red eyes, a snake like a boa-constrictor. Michael was battling him and winning. Once the snake was dead everything in the vision went sort of dark and foggy. Then I started to hear, "Holy, Holy, Holy, Lord God Almighty!" Over and over.

I continued to hear the "Holies", and I decided to join in. As I repeated that phrase along with whoever else was repeating it, I started to see clearer and clearer. I came to realize I was in the throne room of God! I saw steps leading up to God's throne. I saw twenty-four golden thrones, decorated with precious stones, kings sat upon them wearing very ornate crowns. And the living creatures flying overhead kept declaring God's holiness.

I could not get up off the floor before the throne. But I could see pretty well what was going on in front of me. Behind me I knew there was a great multitude, but I never saw them because I was at the front of the congregation. I didn't know for sure if they were angels or people. Suddenly I started repenting. I wept and I said, "I am sorry Lord. I never knew how real this all was." I continued to repent, "Lord I am so sorry. I didn't know." I must have repeated the same general apology twenty times. And then, for no apparent reason, one of the kings fell down before God's throne and started to worship. One by one, in no particular order, the kings all went down, throwing down their crowns and worshipping God and His Lamb.

All the people throughout the throne room started to worship. The noise grew louder and louder until all of the sudden everyone, including the living creatures, went completely silent. I looked up as best as I could to see what had happened, to see what had caused this sudden silence. It was Jesus! He had just walked out from the right side of the throne! The whole room, we were struck in awe, none of us could say a word!

As Jesus walked down the steps, He came towards me and all of heaven started shouting, "Glory to the Lamb of God!"

"Jesus has come!" "Praise His Holy Name!" "Worthy is the Lamb who was slain!" As they all shouted I watched as Jesus walked over to me!

The weight of His glory was so heavy I couldn't even look up. When He put His hand on my left shoulder I could only kneel next to Him. I rested the left side of my face on His left leg as He stood next to me. Many things were happening around me that were difficult to either understand or see. They seemed to be talking about me. And it was as if I was involved with some kind of a ceremony. All I knew was that I was being commissioned and sent out. Jesus said, "Wherever I send you these two angels will go with you." Just then I saw two angels fly out from the other side of the throne and high up into the air, each one landing behind me, one to my right and the other to my left. Jesus said, "They are Hope and Mercy. They are going with you wherever you go."

Many more things happened while I was there but I don't understand them very well and it's hard to describe. After what felt like a lifetime, I was back in the room of the birthplace of the Azusa Street Revival. I was completely out of my vision now, but still so overwhelmed with the glory of God that it was hard to get up off the floor.

God wanted to show me how literally He had just deposited His glory into me, and He said, "Pray for Ricardo." Ricardo was a friend of Rodney's who had met us there. Ricardo was a retired professional Thai-Kick Boxer, very stoic as you would imagine the personality of a kick boxer to be. As I hugged him and started to pray, he wept like a seven-year-old little boy, the love of God was pouring into him. Next I grabbed Rodney's hand and Rodney fell to his knees weeping. It was so real! I was dripping with the glory of God!

Then God told me to anoint everyone in the room. He gave me specific instructions on how to pray. But when I told Thomas, he refused. He said, "Not now." And he resisted me. The Holy Ghost was grieved. I asked him again maybe ten minutes later, but he refused again. Then I was grieving so terribly I just wanted to leave. What an overwhelming way to end such a moment with God!

I could hardly talk for the next couple days, I was drained and sort of feeling drunk . . .

Δ   Ω

My life was forever changed at the Bonnie Brae house. The reality of the kingdom of God was imparted to me in a way I cannot even explain. God is literally seated upon a throne! And He loves us! He is alive and in heaven right now watching over us.

This message of God's love has only increased over the years. When I was a child I knew His love the way a child knows His love, but as I became a man I came to know His love more fully. I continue to search so I might know the bottomless riches of His unending love for me (for us).

It was only a few months later that dad died and I left California. I was grieving, watching many lives, not only my dad's, falling into judgment. I said "Goodbye" to my mother, brothers and sisters and explained to them that I might not be coming home for a long time. When I got to Arizona I witnessed more judgment. Then Ken, my dearest friend, got hurt. I am partly to blame. (I should have been a better friend but I was not.) Ken's arm ending up being broken in three places; I will never forget that night taking him to the hospital and feeling incredibly guilty. Ken had been a phenomenal friend for me; I was only a mediocre friend for him.

I left Arizona with much sadness and regret, but I had to continue to obey the Lord. I passed through Indianapolis to be with my biological father for Christmas, and I was thinking about leaving for Africa from Detroit. That was the worst trip ever, being with dad. It felt like we fought the whole three months I was there. We both said many things we later regretted. It was proving to be very difficult to leave the states.

I passed through Kansas City to visit a "house of prayer" and then onward to Arkansas to be back with Casey. I had no money to fly to Africa and God kept slowing my departure. It was very good to see Casey; God was about to do another miracle for him. Casey to this day, refers to me as his "rabbit's foot" – I will tell you why.

Casey picked me up in Kansas City and drove me back to his place in Arkansas. Casey had gotten himself engaged. He was telling me the whole story and catching me up on the years of news I had missed being away from Arkansas. He asked me to pray, "I entered this contest" he explained, "the winner gets to propose to his fiancée, live at halftime during the Superbowl!" He went on to explain that the winner also gets money, plane tickets, a ring and a dress. It was a package worth over $15,000. He said, "I'm sure if you pray I will win."

Now, I am definitely not saying that I am some good luck charm, but for Casey I sure seemed to be. Wouldn't you know it, he won the contest! It was surreal. I was sitting next to him during the halftime show on live television as he got down on one knee and proposed to his soon-to-be wife, Katie. It was quite a fun time to be with them. God sure can be romantic! Casey and Katie are married to this day and living very blessed with children. Praise the Lord!

God did many other miracles as I passed through North Carolina, Washington, DC, and Baltimore, on to New York. Along the way something terrible happened. I ended up staying with a Christian author whom I had met at the Kansas City House of Prayer; he was not affiliated with them but just visiting like I was. He enjoyed my testimony and invited me to visit his home on my way out of the country. I didn't think it was going to happen, but then Gary, from Arizona, just happened to be driving past his house. So I had my ride for free, and I was getting that much closer to my destination.

I ended up at the Christian author's home when he and his wife were out-of-town, but he had extended his hospitality to me, so I was staying there a few days until they returned. We became closer friends even though we came from very different backgrounds. But then one afternoon his wife was gone for the day, and he invited me down into the basement. He asked for me to give him a massage since his back hurt so badly. I was quite uncomfortable massaging a man (with oil) and I told him so. But I felt sort of obligated and he continued to push me, so I forced myself to do it.

He was acting stranger and stranger and then he practically forced me to let him massage me too! Ugh. It was so uncomfortable. I just kept praying, "Lord, please don't let anything strange happen." Then he started to rub closer to places men shouldn't massage men and so I jumped up and told him to stop. He asked me why I was *making this so weird.* I was really trying not to be angry with him. It was very clear to me now what his intentions were.

After that happened I was in quite an uncomfortable position, I hadn't any money to leave and I saw no door opened by God. I was stuck at his house another ten days or so. It was incredibly awkward. Not only was he a Christian author but he was also the elder of a church, a business owner, a father, a grandfather and of course a husband. What was I to do? He continued to act like nothing had happened and this was making me even more upset. I avoided him as best as I could.

Then one day I heard the Lord. He said, "How many times did you do similar things to seduce a woman?" The Lord was, of course, right. Who was I to be so mad at this man for his sin and the wrong he had done to me. I had certainly done the same if not worse to many women. So I decided to work on forgiving him. It's a much longer story but I departed from him, grieving. But at least I was able to forgive him. Thanks be to God!

And that became the tone for the six months it took me to leave the US. I was grieving. I was grieving my dad's untimely death, I was grieving the brokenness of the church in America, I was grieving never having known my real dad and the hurt associated with that. I was grieving the bad choices I had made at different points throughout my life. My heart hurt. That's what it feels like to grieve. And that's how I left America and arrived in Switzerland.

Δ   Ω

I had put together enough money to get to Zurich, so I guess that you could say I was meandering my way to Africa. My trip to Switzerland surprised me to say the least. God put me together with a wonderful man named Stephan. Stephan seemed to be grieving much like me. Looking back, it was a very special, quick, two months together. Stephan saw the same problems in the church that I was seeing, and he too was/is a writer, an incredible writer in fact.

I was used to hype and pizzazz coming from teachers and leaders within the church. Stephan had none of this. His humility made it very hard to tell if or when he was ever intending to teach something. I learned a lot by being around him. We talked at length about our fathers and our trying to come to terms with the pain we still carried. We shared at length about the brokenness of this religion called Christianity, and he even took me to a "House Church" conference, speaking to this very issue. There were thirty or so nations gathered at the conference. So we were not alone in what we saw God doing. God was in fact tearing down the religion and I saw it now with my own two eyes! I was not alone in what He had given to me.

Of all the gifts that I received from Stephan, my favorite was his teaching about "Coming to the table with Jesus." He had this simple house church that would start with a meal, like a family, together. At most there would be twenty of us gathered around *The Lord's Table*, and we would *feast* upon *His goodness*. We would remember what Christ did for us on the cross and elaborate about what He has done since. I can still see the faces of the people gathered around that table. I can still remember the pasta dish Prisca, Stephan's wife, cooked the first evening we gathered together. It was a very intimate and special time. Looking back, it was a time of healing for me. Just the time I needed to prepare for all that would come next.

They blessed me in many ways and then I was off to Israel. I was praying late one night/early morning and the Lord told me that He was sending me next to Jerusalem, but He made it very clear that I was not to go anywhere else in Europe. I departed from Stephan and his beautiful family: Prisca, Dylan and Selena, with great difficulty and made my way to Jerusalem.

I had never before thought or dreamed of traveling the way I did. I never really had this great longing to go to Jerusalem or any of these places before God told me to go there. I had become rather content in my late 20's, merely obeying the leading of the Lord, traveling just as He led me, knowing that He always wants to bless me/us.

Arriving in Israel and then Jerusalem was like something out of a dream. My flight landed exactly 7:00 a.m., July (the 7th month) on the 7th day.

It was absolutely the Lord sending me to The Holy Land!

Chapter 12

On the flight to Jerusalem I sat next to a U.S. military man, a battle proven soldier. Before we landed I was able to get some pretty awesome stories out of him about his time in Iraq and Afghanistan. He inspired me, so once I got to Jerusalem I wrote a post on my blog entitled, "Warrior Priests". It was an awesome revelation about our true identity in Christ, as both holy men and spiritual warriors.

I will never forget the flight to Tel Aviv. The soldier told me that he was on his way to Israel for a wedding. For whatever the reason, when he started to tell me about the wedding, I realized that most everyone around us was quietly listening to our conversation. I must say it was pretty good conversation. But as he talked about the wedding, one by one everyone around us told us that they too were on their way to Israel for a wedding. It was so odd. Literally every single seat that was filled in front of me, to my left, right and the entire row behind me, were all going to Israel for a wedding! Do you get the significance yet? In Christ, we are *all* on our Way to The Promised Land of God for a Great Wedding, The Wedding of the Lamb! So exciting! I got off the plane in a daze, things were happening so incredibly.

Throughout the first couple of days after I arrived in Israel I was greeted no less than five times, "Welcome Home!" I thought it a very strange greeting but then it just kept happening. I didn't think that I looked very Jewish. I didn't understand why so many of the Israelis were greeting me that way. Finally the sixth or maybe seventh time I was greeted that way by a bus driver, I wept. I realized I *was* in fact home. I was in the Holy Land of my God, the land where I will dwell with Him one day when He returns to reign on the earth. My Father wanted me to know that He had brought me home. God did so many special things for me upon my arrival to The Holy Land. It was a very special time.

There are so many stories to tell about my time in Israel. I am going to really have to listen to the voice of God in sharing what He wants me to share so that this doesn't become a book within a book. That first trip to Israel was not about me ministering for the Lord, but rather Him ministering to me. He did so many very personal things for me while I was there. Even correcting me; I was fasting and praying and wanting to grow closer to Him, when the Spirit of the Lord led me to a very special place in Galilee. I had no idea what to expect in the Golan, but evening came as I happened upon a military installation. I didn't know they would be there. I was just following the leading of the Lord. They turned me away, but it was so late in the evening I would have had nowhere to go in the middle of the night since the buses had stopped running.

This one soldier who spoke pretty good English told me that he would get approval for me to sleep in their bunker at the foot of their encampment. I was very glad, the idea of walking in the pitch black throughout the Golan without a flashlight did not sound very attractive to me, especially because I was so weak from traveling all that day. Night fell, they got approval for me to stay and in no time I was completely alone in absolute darkness, inside of an Israeli bunker.

I was afraid of the dark until I was in my late twenties but God had set me free. So now being that alone in the night was actually peaceful. The stars were incredible out there in the middle of nowhere. I felt so very close to God. I fell asleep early on into the night, lying on the hard, crude bench inside of the bunker.

About 4:00 a.m. or so I woke out of a dream, "I was washing dishes next to Brian, my brother. I was washing twice as fast as and much better than he was in the dream. Our dad, Roger was behind us sort of overseeing. I kept rushing Brian along, almost yelling at him, "Keep up!" Just then he dropped a dish and the dish shattered all over the floor. I turned so angry at him for making a mistake, and I started to beat him terribly. I punched him in the face until my hand was bloody and hurting from how much I hit him. His face was all black and blue and bloodied. Then I decided that he had received enough punishment so I went back to washing dishes."

"My dad came over to us. I thought for sure he was going to yell at me for what I had done to Brian but instead he just comforted my brother, saying, "Brian, here let me help you up. Don't worry about Robert. He is just very passionate about his job. He really really wants to make me proud. And he wants everyone else to do excellent as well." Dad cleaned Brian off and he slowly went back to washing dishes. My heart was pumping and I was still very upset in the dream. I remember thinking, "I hope he learned his lesson so that I don't have to do that again." I felt totally justified in the dream. There was no repentance in me at all for how terribly I beat him, over dropping a dish." The dream ended as my dad spoke with Brian comforting him; and then I woke up.

I woke up weeping. It took me several moments to realize where I was, because the dream was so real. I knew what the Lord was showing me in the dream. He was showing me that I was being way too hard on my brothers in Christ and my fellow believers. In my zeal I was really hurting people with my powerful words of criticism and judgment. Slowly I came to remember where I was and I rolled off the rock solid bench to get down on my knees weeping; I needed to repent. I said, "I am sorry Lord. I am so sorry. I didn't know what I was doing." I vowed before Him as the sun came up that morning, that I would learn to be a true *Warrior Priest*—a *Warrior of Love*.

God is still changing me to this day; into a true soldier, bringing His love into a broken and dying world. Not merely criticizing, but loving, giving truth in love and being patient with how I share what the Lord has given me. It's a long journey to become a true minister of the kingdom of God.

Δ Ω

Some days after I returned to Jerusalem, I was invited to visit the West Bank with an American friend of mine. At that time there was much peace in Israel, it had been five years since the last war with Lebanon, and a while since the last Palestinian Infantada. Israel truly had peace on all her borders. Every year they were breaking the previous year's record for tourism, so I prayed and decided that I was safe, the Lord was with me. We ended up going to a very radical town in the North, ancient Shechem, which today, is called *Nablus.*

We were hosted by a lovely Muslim family in a village just outside of Nablus. We were treated like royalty. Arab hospitality is truly world renown. I have only found a few places that can even come close to competing. For three or four days we were lavished with gifts, food, and anything that we could possibly be interested in about their culture.

One day we were given a very special tour of hidden places throughout the ancient city. Some students from the college wanted to show us *the real* Nablus. We went to a very impoverished refugee camp and listened to many of their very sad stories. We went through all of these back streets and alleyways, seeing many things tourists never get to see. As the day passed it became harder and harder to stay quiet, listening to the horrors of a conflict that has lasted generations, or more accurately centuries.

There was a certain student who was leading the tour. All the others tended to look up to him for leadership. After many hours of listening to what he felt the Israeli's had done to his people and hearing their point of view—I could hear no more. It was too hard on my heart. The suffering of his people and the difficulty of the situation was too tragic and uncomfortable to think about anymore.

Finally, I spoke up, "By any chance, will there be a time for me to share? I have been listening to you and your friends for many hours it would be nice if I had a chance to share." He happily agreed and took me to have tea at a very ornately decorated, ancient-looking Arab restaurant. I was so engaged in the conversation while we were there I was completely unable to enjoy my surroundings or the awesome food.

I told him, "Friend, I hear your story and the struggle of your people. It grieves me to hear how so many of you have suffered. I am sure it grieves God. I would like to offer a suggestion that may help. You come from a world at war and it's all you have ever known, right?" He agreed without argument. I continued, "Let me promise you something. If you continue to be angry and hold to your bitterness against the Israeli's, and I am not talking about your rights, I am talking about your life, if you continue to seek vengeance for all that they have done to you, you will be bitter for the rest of your life. And what will come of your children. Chances are, they will be bitter like their father. And their children what will come of them? Bitterness surely. Unless someone chooses to forgive the offenses, seek a different way and let it go, no one in your family will be free, ever. And the same goes for the Israeli's also."

He listened intently and was very quiet. His response was shocking. He agreed across the board. His friends had slowly left us alone. We were together with only the closest of his friends, and he admitted to me that he had thought similarly about this. He really wanted to be a poet, he didn't want to be a political activist, but his father thrust him into it. He shared some of his poetry with me. It was much better than anything I had ever written, without a doubt. I urged him to get out and see the world, to write and see what was beyond the only *world-at-war* he knew. We grew very close that Saturday we spent together.

The day ended with my American friend and I up on top of a mountain singing worship songs common to us in America; we were praising God while overlooking an incredible view as the sun set over the Mediterranean in the distance. Five or six Palestinian young people watched us praising God, hands lifted high and they would not let us stop singing. Nearly every one of those Palestinian youths had tears in their eyes as we sang to Jesus in front of them. Later on I was told by that young Palestinian leader, listening to us sing atop that mountain was the most spiritual experience he had ever had in his life. It's hard not to let a tear fall thinking of him. Even though we were worlds apart, we really grew to love each other that day. It was a day I will never forget . . . in Ancient Shechem.

Δ   Ω

I felt extremely close to the Lord while I was in Israel. I never had money, but God did miracle after miracle, providing *daily bread* for me. It's such a long story, but I had gotten connected to these Rabbis on top of Mount Zion, just outside the Old City of Jerusalem. It was a family of Rabbis, eight brothers, all Rabbis and somehow I had become friends with the youngest of the brothers. I ended up sleeping in their Yeshiva for several nights when I had nowhere to sleep. It was a great occasion to learn about modern day Orthodox Judaism. I was in fact raised by a Jew. But all those years I had learned very little about the religion he was born into. God did many things while I was there; both to teach me and to give me many lifelong Israeli friends.

It was very difficult staying there because I was not interested in converting. They encouraged me that I would be a tremendous Jew. It was quite the time sleeping at the Yeshiva. They obviously hated the fact that I had a New Testament of the Holy Bible with me and that I would read it often around the Yeshiva. One Sabbath morning I could not take it anymore. I went to a certain prayer room to seek the Lord, because I wanted so badly to leave. I had not one dollar or Shekel to my name. I was praying while looking at the great view of Mount Zion across the valley when the woman overseeing that morning's prayer time came over and started to enquire about my life. I told her some of my very long story. She listened intently.

The Spirit of the Lord came on us both, she said, "This is what the Lord is telling me. I am a widow and you are one of God's servants. I will be like the widow who helped Elijah and give you the last of what I have." And this beautiful child of God gave me her last 50 or 100 Shekels. I, of course, wept as she explained to me, "By faith I believe that this money will last you for the remainder of your trip in Israel and *all* your needs will be met, even in abundance. And God will also provide for me, just like He provided for Elijah's widow." She told me about a certain guest house where she really thought I should stay. I agreed and left for the guest house immediately, very much ready for a good night's sleep.

The fee at the guest house for a night was more than the amount that she had given to me, but the inn keeper was immediately kind to me and accepted the shekels that I had for the room. I would be sharing a room with someone else. When I got to the room and started to unpack my things and prepare to clean myself up (I hadn't showered at the Yeshiva in a couple days because the bathroom was so filthy!) I met my new best friend, a German named Matthias.

Matthias, within thirty seconds of talking with me asked me, "Are you a Christian." I responded, "I am a child of God in Jesus name." He understood exactly why I responded the way I did and we became best of friends immediately. As the story goes, Matthias had come to Jerusalem to rededicate his life to the Lord. He had lived a very sinful life in Germany, he had been a drug dealer and a very bad man, but that was all over now and he wanted to walk with God again. It was a miracle. Another real Jesus miracle! Let me explain why:

Matthias explained to me that his trip would be over in three weeks. He had been in Israel for over two months. He had been praying and seeking the Lord for guidance, but nothing had happened. He was very discouraged because he was really expecting God to do something miraculous to show him that He was forgiven, and that God would receive him. But in all that time nothing had happened, until today.

Within a short time, we were atop the roof of that guest house in the Old City, becoming the best of friends as I shared and shared with Matthias about the love of God. He was a wide open book. God had showed up. He had the miracle he was looking for; and I was it. I told Matthias about my life and testimony with Jesus, and he shared his. He had been exposed to the things of God as a child in Germany, but had started dealing drugs at age fifteen; he was in his thirties when we were together in Jerusalem.

We became inseparable. For his last three weeks in Israel we did everything together. We went on many Jesus adventures together and saw much of the country. We stayed at a very influential Palestinian's house in East Jerusalem and met people from all over the world at that home. The Palestinian Haj and I became friends. We still are. And to make matters even more miraculous with Matthias, one morning he told me, "God told me that I am supposed to pay for the remainder of your time in Israel. You won't be paying for anything. If you need anything, just ask okay?"

I had one month more in Israel when Matthias left. It was a very sad departure. But I vowed to visit him in Germany one day. We have been friends ever since. Matthias is married now and they started a church out of his home, last I heard. God changed Matthias' life forever as he sought after his *Father*. I have to say, my life changed also while I watched Matthias being reunited with Jesus. It was awesome! God did all this to go after one sheep who had wandered astray!

What a Good and Loving Father we have!

Δ   Ω

Matthias left me with a pocket full of money for the remainder of my trip. That first visit to Israel was a very emotional, exciting, and difficult time. I ministered to a girl who kept trying to kill herself while I was there. It was very sad. But she lived. God has done many terrific things with her since we were together. She was reunited with her mom and is doing much better last I heard. She had a very sad life: her father was a very powerful political man in the US and a satan worshipper! She lived with a lot of fear but Jesus overcame much of that while we were together.

I visited the ancient site of Gomorrah and played a bit in the Dead Sea. I met many other Christians, Jews and Muslims throughout Israel, learning much about that amazing and complicated place. Some other very good friends I made were Mennonites, living in the Old City. They were a joy to fellowship with, and be encouraged by. But it was nearing the time for me to go to Africa. Another believer ended up paying my way to fly to Nairobi, Kenya, and the day of my departure came.

Of all the incredible things that happened, listen to how I left Israel:

In an earlier chapter I briefly mentioned about my friend the archeologist whom I tried to get on the Oprah Show. Well, he just so happened to be in Israel the same time that I was there. And what was he doing? Digging for the Ark of the Covenant! It's an incredible story!

I was able to spend a few hours with his team below ground as they were working to find, what they believe was found in the 80's, *The Ark of the Covenant.* One of the volunteers gave me several pieces of ancient pottery as a token for my trip, but I had to leave in a hurry. My flight was departing from Amman, Jordan later that day. I would miss my bus if I spent any more time with them underground. It was so hard to leave! The Lord practically had to drag me out of Israel.

As the bus drove us through the Israel-Jordan border I couldn't help but feel sorrow. To this day I have never felt more at home anywhere in the whole world! I was at home in the Holy Land but I was also a soldier marching to orders and it was time from me to leave. I moped thru the airport in Amman and boarded my plane.

The flights to Africa were surprisingly smooth. I didn't meet anyone on the flights to speak of, so I prayed and readied myself for what would come next in East Africa. I readied myself as much as I could. I knew no one in Africa, but one man I had emailed with a month earlier just so happened to be flying thru Nairobi and was at the airport the same time I was. He would become my escort to the town the Lord was directing me to in West Kenya.

I hadn't the slightest idea what was in store for me in Africa . . .

Chapter 13

I arrived in Africa with $90 USD to my name and no monthly financial support. I had emailed back and forth with one pastor, but other than that I hadn't spoken with him on the phone or really connected with him. Much to my surprise he happened to be in Nairobi at the same time I was. He had already bought the ticket for my flight so he could escort me to his hometown in West Kenya. After repaying the pastor for the flight I was almost out of money again. But the Lord was clearly making a way for me.

I had wanted to visit an orphanage or two in Kenya. This pastor ran several orphanages, but the Lord directed me to a different one out in the countryside. I arrived as clueless as one could be about Africa, the culture and the way their society works, but God was with me. Everything about Africa was foreign to me. Perhaps that seems funny to say but Israel and Switzerland had so many similarities with the US that the difference in culture wasn't so dramatic as it was in Africa. It just hadn't occurred to me how different everything would be in other parts of the world. The Arab and Jewish worlds were certainly different, but western culture had been around in those places long enough that we could communicate and understand one another. Africa, however, was a whole other story to me.

Arriving at the orphanage, owned by a woman named Emily, I couldn't have been less prepared. But immediately I fell in love with the kids. They won my heart within days of being there. Several of the children were sick, a couple where at the point of death, literally. One girl, Mercy, was frighteningly ill, her eyes completely filled with blood, so much so, that there was no part of them white, only blood red. Another precious girl,

Melody (everyone called her Mello), had so many worms inside that her stomach was the size of a soccer ball. Mello was about six years old, but was so small she looked about 2 or 3. These two little girls, Mercy and Mello captured my heart from the first day I arrived.

There were others who were quite sick, and on the second day after I arrived, I started to pray for everyone in Jesus name. Five of the seven sick kids were healed immediately but Mercy and Mello seemed to be totally unaffected by the prayers. I prayed that night that the Lord would reveal to me why they weren't healed. The next day Emily arrived at the orphanage and while we were speaking with one of the children we learned that Mercy had had a spell put on her! The local/village witch had been cursing the orphanage and the children who lived there for some time. I later learned that she did not like Emily at all, she didn't like the orphanage, and so acting like something of a judge, she was putting a curse on the place.

I prayed, "Lord, what do I do now?" The Lord simply said, "Just baptize her and the spell will be broken." As I was preparing to baptize Mercy, I decided to baptize Mello also. When the other children and workers of the orphanage caught wind of what I was doing, everyone wanted to be baptized in Jesus name, even several of the neighbors! None of them wanted to go to the river for fear of snakes so we got a large wash basin and filled it with water. I baptized something like 50 people that day. It was a time of great joy and celebration! Everyone was so happy!

And the best news was that Mercy was healed within hours of the baptism! It still brings a tear to my eyes thinking of her. I can still see her blood-red eyes, but then I watched as the white part returned slowly, within hours of the baptism. Within two or three days her eyes were completely white again, shining brightly, and her deathly cough was gone. Jesus healed her! I got to baptize her but Jesus had done this incredible, very notable miracle. Word quickly spread about the young American missionary that God was listening to.

As word spread, pastors and other men of influence started to come looking for me at the orphanage. They wanted me to preach and travel with them but I was content to remain with the kids. More and more sick people were coming to find me, I would pray for them and God would heal every one of them!! It was like something out of the book of Acts! But then I felt I couldn't remain there any longer. It really seemed that it was time for me to go to Uganda to fulfill the original Word of the Lord! Even though so many exciting things were happening in Kenya, I left after being at Emily's orphanage for one month.

I left hoping to return to them; it was a very difficult departure. Many of the kids wept and wept as I went away. One boy who got especially close to me, Daniel (another Daniel) must have wept for an hour as I was preparing my things to leave. I can still remember many of their names, Daniel, Solomon, Clinton, Obama (his real name was Eddie but they called him Obama because he looked like a young Barack Obama), Mercy, Mello, Stacey, Helen, Cynthia . . . I can still see their faces.

It was so precious to see them weep as I left. It made me feel like they loved me in the same way that I loved them. As hard as it was to leave I had to continue to follow the leading of the Lord.

Δ   Ω

Arriving in Uganda was like arriving at the front lines of a terrible battle. The spiritual warfare I encountered immediately, was like nothing I had ever experienced before. That man who had first emailed me, Unity connected me with a local pastor. I never figured out why I was not invited to stay with Unity. In fact, I was never allowed to see his home. It made me feel uncomfortable at times, trying to figure out what these men were doing with me? There were many strange things happening to me at the hands of my hosts, and it got stranger by the day. I had to fight that feeling of fear and paranoia nearly every day. Looking back I probably didn't pray nearly as much as I needed to while ministering in Uganda.

Many personal things happened while in Uganda. Those things would help to explain the intensity of the spiritual warfare. If you ask me about these things when we are together, I will explain in greater detail. But I preached often throughout the outskirts of Kampala, and every time my sermons were accompanied by a very heavy spiritual struggle. Along with terrible dreams and troubled sleep, I had a difficult time focusing during my sermons. I had a very hard time trusting those pastors... and it got worse and worse, day by day. It was as if I had a large blinking money sign on my head and many of those pastors were bucking for who would win the *prize*. Over and over, I tried to convince them that I was, in fact, broke, but they would not listen. I tried to encourage them by saying, "The kingdom of God is all the riches we need." But they were not *receiving* this word: they were often maneuvering in hopes that I was playing some kind of a game with them. It was uncomfortable, making it hard to get close with any of them.

It all came to a head about three weeks into my trip when one day I began to experience diarrhea. If you are from Africa, you know that diarrhea is a horrible sign. Usually having terrible bad case of diarrhea means Malaria; and upwards of 30-40% of the people who get Malaria in Africa, especially Uganda, they die. In fact, I had preached at a pastor's funeral in Kenya who suddenly died of malaria while he was driving. He didn't even have a fever when his liver failed. Malaria is a terrible sickness! Within a day of having this diarrhea it was confirmed by these men, I had malaria!

I got so weak I couldn't get out of bed. Everything in my body dumped out of me within the first forty-eight hours of getting malaria. I was totally dehydrated, beyond weak, and hardly able to stand by the second day. I remained in bed from that second day on. I was so sick that even if I sat up in bed the whole room would start to spin and I would feel like fainting. It was beyond horrible.

The pastor kept urging me to go to the doctor. He said, "When Africans get Malaria we often die without going to the doctor. But a white man who gets Malaria in Africa and doesn't go to the doctor will die for sure!" I listened, and then I reached across the bed and grabbed my torn Bible from the dollar store back in California. I raised it up and said, "Do you see this Bible?" The pastor said, "Yes." I explained, "All I have in this world I have bet on believing that this Bible is true. I have no money. No business to return to at home. I have no more friends or family because they all think that I have lost my mind, long ago. At this point in my life, if I can't trust that this Bible is true and that God is going to heal me then I would rather die. So please leave me alone. I'm not going to the doctor."

The pastor threatened to take me by force to the hospital, but by the third day he realized I wasn't going to budge. I was so sick that third day I thought to myself, *I really might die from this!* I fell asleep early that day and woke up in the middle of the night to the sound of rain beating down on the sheet metal roof of the house. It's amazingly loud when the rain beats on the metal roofs in Africa. I lay there thinking for quite some time. What it would be like to die? After a long series of debates within myself, I concluded that even though I was still so sinful Jesus would save me, so I wasn't afraid about going to hell. But I decided that I probably wouldn't be much to speak of in heaven. I thought to myself, *the Lord knows how much I enjoy gardening so maybe I will be a gardener in heaven, beautifying the city streets of gold and perhaps growing gardens out in paradise?* I must have laid there for an hour thinking on these things.

In the midst of all this musing, the Lord suddenly showed up! He said, and rather comically I might add, "What kind of a story do you think it would be if I let you die in Africa?" I had to laugh it was such a funny question. I responded while chuckling, "It would be a terrible story Lord. The story would sound like this, Robert, having left all his family and friends and business behind, to follow what he believed was God's plan for him to go to Africa, was killed of malaria." I laughed, "Yeah. That would be a horrible story, Lord. Not so inspiring . . ." The Lord smiled at me and said, "So of course I am going to heal you."

Such peace came over me and I couldn't help but weep. My Savior had come for me!

Suddenly the power of God came on my body like nothing I had ever experienced before! The power was almost too much! At one point I literally said, "Can I handle this Lord! It feels like I'm either going to lift off of this bed or I am going to explode!" After I said that the power began to slowly subside. Once it was gone, I sat up for the first time in 2 or 3 days and the room didn't spin anymore. I got out of bed and I was not weak or light-headed. I raised my hands high and I started to praise His holy name! "You healed me!" I said. "I'm sorry I had doubts, Lord . . ." And I wept and praised Jesus, my Salvation and my Hope, because of His unending love and His limitless mercy.

I was saved, again. "O the wonders of our gracious and compassionate Savior! Jesus! Who holds us as if in the palm of His hand!" I was finally starting to believe in Him. After all these years and stories with my God, I was finally believing, God loves me! My life has changed again. Everything I had thought about God changed again. Uganda turned out to be one of the most life changing times I have ever had with God, ever!

$$\Delta \quad \Omega$$

Now this might be a little hard for you to swallow, but when I got Malaria in Uganda it was the first time in something like 11 or 12 years I had been sick. I was sick sometime in 1999 and then a small flu or something in 2000, but after that, no sickness whatsoever, not even a tooth ache until 2012. God is *able*! It wasn't anything I did either, because I was plenty sinful throughout my early twenties. All the glory is to God! Our lives are truly in His hands.

After my healing from malaria, I knew that I had to leave Uganda right away. Those pastors had acted so strangely, and my friendship with them was plummeting downhill so quickly that I knew I had to leave before something else terrible happened. On my way out of town I happened to run into another pastor, a man who ran a school, an orphanage and a church. I had preached at his place a couple weeks earlier. He and his wife explained to me that the place I had been living was home to some of the best known witches in all of Uganda. They were explaining to me that many other witches come from around the country to that village where I was living outside of Kampala, to learn from these chief witches. It turned out I was living in the center of a great witches-coven! Maybe the devil had plotted to kill me in Uganda. I don't know. But my God is bigger than that guy.

I was nearly back to normal on the bus ride out of Kampala and back to Kenya. I was blowing my nose a lot but within a few days that too was gone and I was totally healed. When I returned to Kenya I had a new found confidence in my Father. And I had a new found confidence in His power. The ministry of the kingdom of God was with me in even greater power as I started to preach at the churches in Kenya. Of all the ministry work I have done up to this point in the story, the most dramatic miracles and awesome sights of His glory that I have seen God work through me were in Kenya after I returned from Uganda.

I started preaching almost immediately upon my return. I prayed for dozens if not a hundred sick people. I only know of one story when someone wasn't healed. That man died (some people call this a form of healing?) I still can see his face as I was praying for him.

This is one of my favorite stories: I was on my way to preach at a wedding (*Yes, They preach at weddings in Africa.*) I was in the car with one of my dear friends, Joshua, who was a pastor and the principal of a high school. He was driving when someone called for prayer. Joshua nonchalantly handed me the phone and said, "Can you pray for this man?" I agreed, took the phone, and said, "Friend, do you believe that Jesus can heal you over a cell phone?" The sick man agreed, "Yes. I do." I said, *"Then in Jesus name, Be healed brother! Get up off your bed and walk!"* I might have said a few more things, but it was a very short prayer. Then this sick man on the other end of the call started shouting and praising Jesus, "Hallelujah! Praise Jesus! Glory be to God!" It was as if he had been healed immediately. I guess the Holy Ghost came upon him?

Some months later when Joshua and I were ministering together elsewhere, he asked me if I remembered praying for this man? After he refreshed my memory he told me the whole story. "Brother Robert," (that's what they usually called me in Africa,) "that man was on his death bed. The doctors had only given him a week or two to live. The diabetes was so bad that the doctors wanted to cut off his legs to save him. He said that he would rather die than live without legs. He was waiting to die when he called me and I put him on the phone with you while on our way to the wedding." Joshua continued, "When you prayed for him, within four days, the swelling went down on his legs. He was totally and completely healed of diabetes. The doctors even called it a miracle; and when he left the hospital he had no kidney problems, no diabetes, no high blood pressure, nothing! He was totally and completely healed."

I have so many stories to share about Africa. And they are all so fun. But I want to tell you about Jack. Jack is one of my favorite people in the whole world. To this day I miss him often. Jack was born and raised to be very religious, *Very Religious*. In his household they knew the Bible backwards and forwards, but they never believed in it, not really. Jack's father even built many churches throughout Kenya, and was a very senior figure within the denomination. But something about their doctrine kept the power of God and the miracle working glory of His Kingdom hidden. When Jack was around 45 years old he was diagnosed with kidney failure, high blood pressure and advanced diabetes. Jack owned a hospital in Kenya at the time. The doctors who worked for him all agreed that he would be dead within six months or so.

Jack started to get his affairs in order. He was finalizing his will and basically waiting to die when one day, he decided, *well if I am going to die at least I can enjoy my time drinking beer.* Jack loved beer so he went to the ATM machine to get some money to buy a case of his favorite beer and enjoy it before he died.

While in line at the ATM machine Jack over heard one man preaching to the man in front of him; he was telling him about the power Jesus has to heal people. Jack listened a while and became rather upset, finally interrupting the man who was preaching, Jack said, "What Jesus are you talking about? I have known who Jesus is my whole life, but I have never heard of this Jesus before?" The preacher man told Jack all about Jesus' power to heal. He told Jack, "Jesus is alive! Don't you know?" Jack listened intently. The preacher man invited Jack to go with him immediately and visit his pastor, Joshua. (This Joshua also would become a dear friend of mine.)

Joshua, the pastor, was working in a grimy rather small, metal shop, welding something when Jack arrived. As he heard Jacks story, he sat Jack down and started to tell him about the reality of Jesus and His power to heal. Since he had nothing to lose Jack listened with an open mind. The pastor had Jack confess his many sins. And once Jack had repented, the pastor prayed for him. Jack said something like lightning shot through his whole body, and power surged all up and down him. He fell to his knees, weeping and praising God. Jack went home that night and threw away all his medications. His wife thought he had lost his mind.

After a week or so without the medication, Jack was still alive. His wife was very worried about his condition and the fact that he was refusing to take any medication. So Jack went to the hospital for a checkup. A week after Joshua, the pastor, had prayed for Jack, the doctors pronounced Jack 100% healed. No diabetes. No kidney failure. No high blood pressure. One-Hundred percent healed! And his heart was beating like an 18-year-old for the first time in years. Jack's whole life was forever changed. He would never think, act or live the same again. Jack had met the real Jesus!

Jack and I went on many adventures together throughout West Kenya! We are still very close brothers in the Lord to this day. I love him dearly.

Δ   Ω

On one adventure with Jack we went to see a young man. He was about 22 years old or so, and he had been very sick for three or four years. He was so sick that he would sleep sometimes 20-22 hours a day. He never had normal strength and so he slept all the time; the sickness resembled something like mononucleosis (mono), but that was never the diagnosis. The family sold their land and many of their possessions to try to find and afford a doctor who could help him. But none of the doctors could even figure out what was wrong with him. It was a great mystery that continued year after year as he got worse and worse.

Jack knew the young man's older brother, John. John convinced Jack and I to go and pray for his little brother one day. The three of us traveled much further than John had originally told us that we were going but I wasn't upset. We took a bus some two hours outside of town then had to walk another two hours or more back to the village where John's brother lived with his mother. When we finally arrived I just knew that God was going to heal this young man. I was so excited!

The Lord told me to let Jack do the talking; I was sort of leading from the rear. We followed what the Lord told us to do and then finally prayed for the young guy. The miracle happened immediately. He was blasted by the power of God and his mother also. The mother continued weeping even as we left the house. The once sick young man felt so good that he walked us all the way to the road where we could catch our bus back to town. He hadn't walked to that road in years. The last thing I heard was that John and his little brother had become preachers around that part of Kenya and the two of them often went around praying for the sick; healing many in Jesus name.

I have to say that it would be hard even for me to believe all of this story except for that I personally lived it. God is so good! He is way better than any of us realize!

Jack had introduced me to a very dear Maasai brother in the Lord. His name is Moses. Moses and Jack became two of the best friends I had ever had in my whole life. I could have lived with Moses far away from town in a little mud hut, with him and his family for the rest of my life . . . and been totally content. Moses and I became even closer. One day he showed me the parcel of ground where he would build for me a home if I ever wanted to stay with him in Africa. Moses and I ministered often throughout our month together in Maasai-land. Moses' testimony is so incredible; I hope one day he writes it down for everyone to read. Moses has seen the powerful hand of God often, he has just as exciting a testimony as me. His tribe kept trying to kill him when he first became a pastor. They were a pagan tribe, worshipping the creation and wanted nothing to do with Jesus. But after the Lord, eight or nine times miraculously kept Moses from harm, everyone in the tribe, including the elders, realized that Moses was in fact God's guy. It is estimated that half of the Maasai are now Christians.

These brothers of mine: Moses, Joshua, Jack, the older Joshua, they were some of the most amazing men of God I had ever met. I was so blessed to have been there with them. It would have been easy to stay in Kenya forever. But my trip would soon come to an end. One night after we were praising God late into the evening with the Maasai children, the Lord came to me in a dream. First He showed me Indonesia, then the Philippines and China, in that order. I knew exactly what I was to be doing in each of those places, and where I was preaching. It was an extremely detailed dream. When I awoke the next early morning, before the sun came up, I prayed and asked the Lord, "Do you really want me to leave Africa?" It was very sad to think of leaving. At that time my friends were going to great lengths to convince me to stay with them.

The next day I got up and prayed, asking the Lord to confirm His word to me. I opened my Bible randomly, to a passage of scripture which said, "The churches in Asia salute you." It was the confirmation I needed. I knew then for certain that the Lord was sending me to Asia. I prayed, "Lord I have no money to get there." Within 24 hours a friend of mine in Arizona emailed me that he had put $500 into my account. The Lord had woke him up in the night and told him the exact dollar amount to give me. It was within $20 of the money I needed to leave Africa.

I continued to preach and visit many places throughout West Kenya as I was making my way to Nairobi. I could write a long book telling of my stories while in Africa. It was very hard on my heart to leave my friends in Kenya. When I went online to purchase my plane ticket to Jakarta, Indonesia the Lord said, "Go back to Israel first", and "I want you to rest. I have things for you to do there before you go to Asia." So I bought a plane ticket back to Amman, Jordan, and I was *on the road again.*

Many unexpected things happened as I was trying to leave Africa. Oddly enough I missed my flight. That is the one of the only flights out of some 500 flights that I have missed throughout my life. I prayed and the Lord told me that He did it on purpose. He wanted me to meet someone. I had one contact in Nairobi, so I called him and he directed me to his home. It would be two more very long and wonderful days in Nairobi until I could finally leave Kenya. While I was in Nairobi I met another dear friend, David; the aptly named Praise and Worship leader. We are friends to this day. But then, with no further ado, I was on my way back to Israel.

I arrived in Jerusalem February 17th . . .

I will never forget that date because of what happened next.

Chapter 14

February 19th, first thing in the morning a friend emailed me and said, "Robert, did you say that God is sending you to Indonesia? Well there is a delegation that just arrived at the house of prayer in Jerusalem from Jakarta. You had better get over there quick!" I rushed down the Mount of Olives where I was staying to get to the other side of the Old City where the prayer room was located. I practically ran passed the garden of Gethsemane, Absalom and King Hezekiah's tombs, and around Mt Zion to the prayer room. I couldn't believe it! (I know that sounds strange after all I had already lived through with the Lord, but it was still always so incredible when He would move.) A whole group of Indonesian saints of God were in fact worshipping the Lord at the prayer room, just 48 hours after I had arrived in Jerusalem. Another Jesus miracle!

These Indonesian believers were preparing the way for the Spirit of God to rain down on their city in May of that year. They were hosting the World Prayer Assembly in Jakarta in May. Several of the organizers for the global gathering had come to Jerusalem to pray in the blessing, to literally "blow the trumpet in Zion!" God made sure that we were both in Jerusalem at the same time and even meeting at the same place!

I met a dear friend named David and another one named Tony that day. I told them my story about the Lord sending me to Indonesia by way of Israel and how I had only flown into Jerusalem 48 hours earlier. I showed them the dreams which had come true that I had written down in my prayer journal, and I showed them the dream I had just had about coming to Indonesia. They were encouraged. They saw it as a sign that the Lord was with them in their preparation for the World Prayer Assembly. It was a tremendous miracle. Both David and Tony urged me to find them whenever I arrived in Jakarta and I never saw them again in Jerusalem; their schedules were already booked. It was confirmed by the miracle working power of God, I was, in fact, on my way to Indonesia!

Over the years God has provided miraculously for me. There have been several different ways He has provided. I have shared some of the stories but I have also worked here and there. This trip to Israel when money got really tight, the door that the Lord opened for me was working with a dear friend of mine, Ron. Ron had a cleaning company and so I rolled up my sleeves, humbled myself and went to work.

One day, while vacuuming and cleaning out a synagogue, I heard this horrible voice start to chide me. It was the enemy for sure, he said, "Why do you serve this God? Look at how He treats His ministers. Here you are supposedly saving the world but He has you reduced to slaving away like a maid. Doesn't sound like a good and loving Father to me!" This devil continued to come against me until finally I responded, "You don't know Him. My Father knows exactly what He is doing! You will see. He is going to make something incredible out of me. Just watch." The devil left me after I rebuked him.

I have worked so many odd jobs along the way. In North Carolina I was a janitor. In New York I was a carpenter and day laborer. I have been a landscaper many times, one time I cleaned the lawns of a cemetery for days on end. I have planted, I don't know how many gardens for people. It hasn't always been very glamorous. I wanted to make a note of this as you are reading these stories. The Lord never led me back into business but many times I have worked, just like Paul, "with my own hands". Sometimes God provided money miraculously without my physical labor but other times He led me to labor. Once I left the country, however, I never had to work, except for helping my friend cleaning synagogues in Israel.

A little humility never hurt anyone, I guess ...

Δ Ω

Back on the Mount of Olives I was to room with Freddy, a dear older man from South Africa. You couldn't have found two men more different than Freddy and me to room together. I was in my 30's and Freddy his 70's. I was trained for white-collar work from a young age, Freddy was a steel-factory worker his whole life, built like a tank and accustomed to a rough life. I had known the Lord since I was a boy and was filled with the Spirit. Freddy had never experienced the baptism of the Holy Spirit and he was much older when the Lord got a hold of him. But we'd each had hard lives in our own way. We both would have loved to have had better childhoods and better fathers. No one would have ever guessed it, and maybe it was just because we were roommates in The Holy City, but Freddy and I became the best of friends, literally overnight.

We were inseparable for many weeks. We shared a bed together and talked late into the night about our lives. He seemed more like an older brother than a father or grandfather figure. Sometimes in fact, it was as if I was the older brother. I really enjoyed Freddy. He was my dear friend from the start. I told him about my recent adventures in Africa and he told me about his lifelong adventures in South Africa. Freddy was good for my heart. I believe I was for his too.

One time I was invited to preach at a church in Bethlehem and I invited Freddy to come with me. We ended up being hosted by a Palestinian nondenominational church; we shared a room the entire week. While we were in Bethlehem I ended up writing much of his life's story down for him. I don't know exactly how it happened but as he was telling me stories one day I felt incredibly impressed to write them down. He clearly needed to get some things off of his chest. I was fascinated by his life, so I wrote as he talked. We started a fast together and sometimes we stayed up through the night, talking and writing.

After a week together in Bethlehem he finally confided in me. "Robert," he said with his burly Afrikaans accent, "I came to

Jerusalem to die." As it turned out he had been diagnosed with a terrible disease (I can't recall the name of it) and the doctors gave him less than 6 months to live. He had gotten his affairs in order back home, said goodbye to his family and came to Jerusalem, ready to die. I guess maybe he didn't feel prepared to depart from this life quite yet and he was letting me help him say goodbye to this world. It was a tremendous gift Freddy gave me. I have rarely ever been trusted with anything so precious. We shed many a tear together as we swapped stories. Freddy's life was clearly one of the roughest I had ever heard of.

Freddy's dad was a terrible, angry drunk. He would drink himself, black-out drunk and do the most horrible things to Freddy's older brother and mother, but Freddy was younger, so it was never quite as bad for him. Freddy's big brother was his hero. He often protected him from his dad. His mom was beaten nearly to death several times, right in front of Freddy. So he lived with the expectation of chaos and pain on a daily basis. It was Freddy's wife who years later brought him to the Lord, but no one had ever helped Freddy to receive healing from the Lord for his heart. There were days that Freddy would weep for hours on end and not want to leave his bed. God was really doing a big work in him. I was watching years of pain, shame, hopeless-ness, and condemnation break off from my friend's heart. God is awesome to watch.

Then one evening after we returned to Jerusalem from Bethlehem, there was a traveling ministry team in town from California. I invited Freddy to attend with me. He was rather unsettled about going, the Holy Spirit stuff sort of made him uncomfortable, but because I wanted him to go so badly he came. We had great joy and celebration during the praise and worship, and then one of the ministers called Freddy out of the crowd to be prayed for. The power of God touched Freddy that night! His life would be forever changed.

Many other things happened during my second trip to Israel. I was nearly beaten by this Orthodox Jew when he invited me over his house for Shabbat (the Sabbath meal). I traveled nearly across the whole country and saw many of the Israeli sites that I hadn't seen on the last trip. It really seemed that the Lord wanted me to rest. So mostly I rested with Freddy and a few others friends, preparing myself for my trip to Indonesia.

The time had come for me to leave for Jakarta. I was able to celebrate Pesach, Passover, in Jerusalem and just after the Holy Days were over, I had my plane ticket to fly into Jakarta. I hurt that I would have to leave Freddy to go to Indonesia.

Leaving Freddy was strange because he suddenly seemed so lively. After spending that week with me in Bethlehem, and then after the Holy Ghost fell upon him back in Jerusalem, Freddy was a changed man. I couldn't put my finger on it until later on when I found out what had happened. Somewhere along the way Freddy had gotten himself healed. God totally healed Freddy! He ended up contacting his family and they purchased him a flight ticket home. The last I heard he was alive and living with his wife back in South Africa. Such amazing stories have I gotten to live through. God healed Freddy's disease, but more so, Freddy met God in a way he never had imagined before. Incredible! What an incredible God we have! He loves us so much!

I continue to thank the Lord for letting me get to know Him so intimately.

Δ   Ω

I would love to say that I arrived in Jakarta to a king's welcome, but No. That was not the case at all. My flight finally landed after 9:00 p.m., and by the time I got my luggage it was after 10:00. When I called Tony and David they were both busy, and it was too late for them to come and get me. They didn't think about me not having any money since Indonesia is so cheap. So they told me to get a hotel and that they would find me the next day.

I don't know why I couldn't tell them I had only $12 to my name. I don't think it was pride. I just wanted to see what awesome things God was going to do next. I was very very tired and it was getting awfully late. This one taxi cab driver told me, "Just sleep in the airport. People do it all the time." That sounded good to me since I could hardly keep my eyes open; I found a bench and fell asleep in minutes.

I awoke at 4:00 a.m. out of a terrible dream. The enemy was near to me as I gathered myself off that bench. He started to say ridiculous things to me like, "Some servant of God! Why are you serving a God who leaves you stranded at the airport? Look at how God treats His children! You really believe He loves you? This doesn't look like love to me . . ." I finally rebuked the devil, he stopped bothering me and he left. I will never forget that morning, wandering the airport, waiting for something to open up so I could get something to eat.

Finally, by 7:00 a.m. I got an email back from my friend David. Around 9:00 a.m. the car he sent for me arrived. I spent the day with David and his brother Mark who had been missionaries in Jakarta for many years. Mark had married a beautiful Indonesian woman some years earlier; he learned the language and became an Indonesian citizen. These brothers opened many doors for me to minister, and suddenly I was preaching and doing the works of God. I have many stories of God's glorious works as I ministered throughout Indonesia.

God healed a man on the spot! He had just had a stroke and the whole left side of his body was paralyzed. He was healed that night and released from the hospital the next day. Totally recovered! I saw many demons cast out, and gave many words of knowledge while I was preaching.

One of my favorite stories was the first evening I preached at my dear friend Edy's church. There was this rather small man who had come up with his wife for prayer. When I saw him I put my hand near to his wife's belly and started to pray that she would have a baby. He fell to the ground and started to weeping and repenting! I didn't understand what was going on. Then he grabbed the microphone and started to yell in Indonesian!

The power of God fell as he yelled into the microphone so much so that I couldn't stand. Then my translator came over to me to tell me what he as saying. This little man was shouting, "Listen to the True Prophet of God, all Indonesia! Do as he says, for God is with him! He is the prophet God has sent!" All I did was pray that his wife would have a child. I was shocked to hear what he was saying.

Well, later I heard the whole story from that small man, his name was Yohanes. He became my translator several times when I preached, and he told me his side of that story. When he had come into the room that night and saw me ministering in Edy's church he was angry and told the Lord, "If this man is truly from You he will know that my wife doesn't have a baby and he will pray for her without me telling him so!" So then, when he came up and I started to pray over her belly, it was exactly the sign he had requested from the Lord to confirm my authenticity. And so he started shouting, "Hear the true prophet of God, All Indonesia!"

Yohanes and I went on several adventures together preaching around the surrounding area of Jakarta. He became a good friend.

Δ   Ω

One morning I was asked to attend a special prayer service for the upcoming World Prayer Assembly. Tony came and picked me up early in the morning at 2:00 a.m. and we went to go pray at a large stadium where the event was to be held the next week. As the prayer meeting ended at around 6:30 a.m. I met a rather odd man who invited me to preach at his church. I asked Tony what he thought and Tony encouraged me to go and preach.

When we finally arrived at this strange pastor's church I really had to control myself. I was so very tired that when I found out that not only was this not his church but also that he wasn't a pastor at all, and therefore I wouldn't be preaching that day; I was furious! I ignored him after that. I didn't even want to look at him. I was so tired. I ended up sleeping on the chairs of the church for a half an hour before the church service began.

When I woke up I saw this beautiful young Indonesian woman walk down the aisle past me to lead Praise and Worship. I have always been a sucker for a woman who can sing, and this

Indonesian princess had an amazing voice. I had to keep from looking at her because I kept reminding myself that I wasn't there to fall in love, but to minister. After Church she came up and introduced herself to me. It turned out that it was her Uncle's church that I had been dragged to that morning and I was asked to share a short testimony.

After church was over that beautiful singer made me a plate of delicious spicy Indonesian food. She sat down next to me as I was ministering to her friend, also on the praise and worship team. I prayed for his back and God healed him instantly. The Indonesian princess was surprised and then she asked me if I would pray for her stomach. Instantly God healed her stomach too. She was shocked. I have to admit that even after all these testimonies I still get surprised and excited watching the Lord move!

All of the sudden several of the old ladies in the church were putting me and Shirley, that beautiful singer, together. They said, "Shirley, go and show Pastor Robert around town. He has never seen the city of Jakarta before. Go and give him a tour." I was so excited! Is this really happening? I thought to myself, am I really about to get a tour of Jakarta from this hot singer? God must really like me! Shirley was tired, but eventually she agreed to take me. The church set us up with two chaperones, the strange man who invited me to church that day, and Shirley's friend whose back God had healed. The four of us got on the bus and we were on our way.

Within minutes of being away from the church Shirley and I were flirting like teenagers. I couldn't help myself. She was just so cute and fun to be around. She had the cutest Indonesian accent when she spoke English and she said the most adorable things. I was so happy to be with her. By the time we reached the mall I was already trying to hold her hand. She seemed to like me pursuing her. When I grabbed her hand and walked next to her, she hesitated several minutes before pulling it away. I was very excited. I was 33 years old and absolutely open to being married whenever the Lord provided that perfect wife for me, even if it was in Indonesia!

That whole day was like something out of a movie. We laughed all day long, ate good food and told our stories; we had such a good time. All throughout the day she kept saying, "You have to remember today." I said, "Of course I am going to remember this day. I will remember it for the rest of my life!" I didn't know that I was prophesying. Shirley said, "What is the date?" It was March 12th. Then she would say, "512. You have to remember." We joked about it several times throughout the day. "5.1.2."

When the evening had come we walked the chaperones to the bus and I went to go put Shirley into a taxi. But by the time we got to the taxi stand the whole mall had been shut down for a parade. We were stranded together alone for another several hours. God is so good to me, I thought to myself. Can this get any better? I started to talk to her about her future and wanted to know where she saw herself going, if she wanted a family, etc. Sure it was bold. But my visa was only good for another month and I was really interested in Shirley.

It was nearly 11:00 when I finally got home. The Indonesians ended up giving me an apartment while I was staying in town and ministering. I couldn't believe it when I saw what was the apartment number was! Did you guess it? Yep. 512! Had it not been the joke of the day I would not have recognized it. God had everything lined up perfectly, to the very day! "What else could this mean?" I told her, "I think we are going to get married!?" Shirley was overwhelmed to say the least. But she never said, "No."

The following Tuesday I went to go and visit her Uncle to talk with him about Shirley. Shirley was not raised with her dad so her uncle was her authority figure. I sat in the small room of her uncle's house trying to figure out what I would say to him. Then finally he made my job very easy, in his very broken English, in front of friends and family all crowded into that small living room, Uncle Danny asked me, "So do you love Shirley, or what?" I gathered myself together, looking around at all those strangers and with all sincerity, I said, "Yes. We fell in love."

Uncle Danny was so happy he leapt to his feet with applause! Shirley practically ran out of the room she was so overwhelmed by what was going on. I started to think, we need to fast and pray about this. But before I could say anything, Shirley came into the room and told everyone, "Lets fast and pray about this and see what the Lord will say." Yet another sign! I was convinced. I was going to marry this girl. But I fasted and prayed anyway.

We agreed to fast and pray for three days to seek God for His answer, my dad joined us in the fast back in Detroit, as did Shirley's mom, Uncle Danny, and a few other people. At the end of the three days I heard the Lord say about 4:00 a.m., "I have opened a door for you. If you want to marry her I will bless it." I was so happy. I was finally going to start my own family. Shirley gave a very similar testimony of the Lord confirming to her that He was with her in marrying me, and we met with Uncle Danny soon thereafter to discuss the wedding.

Before I would let Uncle Danny agree to our plan, I told him, "The only problem in this whole romantic story is that I only have $100 to my name." Weddings in Indonesia are a really big deal. A typical Indonesian wedding could easily run two or three year's wages or upwards of $20,000 USD, or even more. I was proposing with $100, and in Indonesia the man pays for everything. Uncle Danny looked down at the hundred-dollar bill I had in an envelope and laughed, saying, "If you have the faith to believe that God will provide for you, I will believe with you!" And we agreed to have the wedding June 9th, 4 weeks to the day after I had met Shirley! I guess you can say that Shirley and I are a little unique; meeting and marrying in a month.

The many many ways that the Lord provided for us were incredible. We ended up with nearly $6,000 for our wedding. It was another tremendous miracle of His provision. The wedding was beyond overwhelming for me being that none of my family was able to make it and the fact that I had only met my bride four weeks earlier ... but Shirley literally looked like an Indonesian Princess; and she was so happy. I put as many of my fears aside as I could and tried to give her the best wedding ever, all things considered.

We married on the beach. We had invited 60 or 70 people and more than 120 showed up for the wedding. We ran out of food but kept ordering more. It was very exciting but also very draining. I met dozens of her family that I had never seen before. They were for the most part kind and welcoming me into their family but I could tell that there was a question in everyone's mind: are these two for real? I have to admit, those fearful thoughts also showed up in me at the wedding. But the Lord was with us from the beginning so I kept going back to all those miracles that Jesus had done for us, and holding on to that. We left a few days after the wedding for our honeymoon and ministry in the Philippines.

Shirley is the best present God has ever given to me! She is one of the reasons I know for certain that God loves me. It sure has been a wild ride all these years with Jesus.

And now I had a beautiful companion to enjoy it with!

Chapter 15

Iwould love to say that it was a fairytale honeymoon in the Philippines but that would be a lie. It turned out that it was hard for us to be married at first. Shirley and I came from very different backgrounds that functioned very differently. To make matters worse, we were both afraid of marriage: afraid that it wouldn't work out, afraid that we would be abandoned and our hearts broken. From the beginning, that fear seemed to be working against us behind the scenes. We did not have the smoothest first couple of years of marriage. We married and were immediately in the mission field together. I would not encourage this for any of my dear brothers and sisters in the Lord. But even with all those troubles, God's grace was with us.

It proved to be extremely difficult to leave Indonesia. Two days after the wedding, Shirley and I got into a huge argument and had to have friends help us to work through it. Then some ridiculous airport employee tried to stop us at the airport for some formality, he said that we didn't have the appropriate papers for Shirley to leave Indonesia. She almost had to stay at the airport and meet up with me later for our honeymoon. But then the Lord prevailed and suddenly we were on our flight to Manila.

Shirley met her father for the first time when she was seventeen. I was in my early twenties when I met my dad. We both came from the same kind of broken and *religious* families. The details of our pasts were obviously different, but the broken families we came from were the same. We both struggled with fear and with letting our hearts be free to love the other person.

It was an explosive and volatile time as Shirley and I learned to open ourselves up, without fear, and love each other.

Δ   Ω

It was amazing that we *just so happened* to have missionary friends of my family from California, in the Philippines. They were a young, zealous couple serving the churches and the poor throughout Manila. Overnight Nathan, the husband, became my new best friend. Jordan, his wife, and Shirley seemed to get along too. It was such a blessing having found those two.

Even though God wasn't doing miracles like He had had in Africa or Indonesia we were all learning to be the servants of God, together. I was sharing everything the Lord had showed me over the years on the road, and Nathan was very encouraging to me. I was like an older brother for him. I was growing a little weary from a rather long journey. My new brother, Nathan lifted my spirit with his child-like faith and trust in God. It was inspiring for me to be around him. Nathan was exactly the brother I needed and I hope I was the brother that he needed too.

This young couple also helped Shirley and me to be more normal newlyweds. Even though we were on our honeymoon we were also in the mission field. It was not always easy. Shirley was dealing with the emotions of being newly married, leaving her country, leaving her friends and family, learning to be a missionary, and learning to get along with a husband like me. I am certain Shirley is the only woman in the world who could have done it . . . I might be a little biased.

Shirley, like me, had left a white collar, executive type life in Indonesia. She was working in management for BMW Indonesia when we met. Her mom had helped her through university, so Shirley was a highly educated college graduate, in management when I met her. She was a woman of faith too. She left all that for the Lord, to follow this broke man (*of faith?*), around the world. What guts. Shirley had it made. All she had to do was to stay the course and her life would have been incredible; at least financially. So I had my woman of faith now all we needed to do was let

God heal us so that we could love each other. In the Philippines it was like the shock of meeting and marrying so quickly was wearing off and now we were really getting to know each other.

So that dream I had in Africa came true. In the dream *I was in Indonesia preaching in a mall*. I dreamt then, *I was in the Philippines with many church people, playing basketball. And then I was in China touring the country, among other things.* Well, I preached at probably a half a dozen malls in Indonesia where many of the churches rent space in malls throughout the country. I was with a church where I preached in the Philippines while they competed in a church basketball league. Then we did in fact tour almost the entire country of China on trains. That dream the Lord gave me so many months before, had come true. Every single detail. Amazing!

There were not very many signs and wonders that happened during our ministry in the Philippines. Most of what God was doing was with Nathan and me, and within our marriages. I was learning to be a married man and having some time to enjoy my wife while in the Philippines; after all, we were on our honeymoon. In hindsight, I wish I had given Shirley a better honeymoon, but I was such a soldier for the kingdom of God that I wanted to labor for Him (Sorry, Honey). But the Lord did provide us a "honeymoon suite". That's what we called the room above the house where we stayed with Nathan and Jordan. It was beautiful out in the countryside, on the outskirts of Manila. We even had a monkey with us named, Moses. It wasn't a total failure of a honeymoon but it certainly could have been better.

I will tell you a funny story: Nathan and I decided to fast and pray for our time of ministry in the Philippines, and for whatever else the Lord would have us do together. Sometimes when I fast it is very blessed, full of grace and is a time of joy, but this was not one of those times. Be advised: It might not be the best idea to fast during a honeymoon. By the third or fourth day of the fast I was so weak I could hardly stand. It was a Sunday and I had to preach that day, but how on earth was I going to preach without any strength?

We arrived at the church. The church owned a school on the first floor and the sanctuary was up stairs. As I climbed the stairs I was so weak it was hard to hold my head up. I was talking with several people who were much shorter than me so I was looking down when suddenly I smashed my head into a low-hanging air conditioning unit! It was sticking out from the building into the hallway leading to the chapel. It hurt so badly.

I was so dazed by the blow that I thought I was going to pass out. I started to get tunnel vision and a sick feeling in my stomach. I prayed, "Lord you can't let me pass out! They might not let me preach!" I kept thinking, *I can't let anyone know that I am hurt*. So I walked back down the stairs with Shirley to find a place to be alone and stop the blood from running down my face. *I have to shake this off*, I kept thinking. But I was really hurt! My poor wife. The things she has dealt with being married to me.

By the look on Shirley's face I could tell that this wasn't a little cut. I was thinking, *Great, I will probably need to get stitches and maybe a shot for infection*. As these thoughts ran through my mind I decided to ignore them all and to just pray and trust God for my healing. After a few moments I gathered myself, put a cloth on the cut to stop the bleeding and I went inside the church. The service had just begun without us. Shirley and I sat down in the back.

I was too dizzy to stand for praise and worship. I prayed, "Lord, I can't get up, how am I going preach? I need Help." When they introduced me to come up and minister I wobbled as I approached the pulpit but when I grabbed the microphone a sudden surge of energy rushed through my body and I was totally myself again! I preached a lighthearted and joyful sermon, as I remember it, and prophesied about things that the Lord would be performing in His Church; removing *religion* from out of us and replacing it with a genuine faith. I remember really enjoying myself preaching.

At one point during my sermon, the faces on the entire audience changed from smiles to absolute shock and horror! I didn't understand if I had said something wrong or what. I looked at the pastor who was interpreting for me: he was speechless too and had a strange look on his face. *What on earth did I do?* I wondered. Then Jordan jumped up from her seat, came over to me and wiped the blood from off of my face.

It turned out that while I was preaching the gash on my head had opened up again and blood was streaming down the side of my face. It must have been quite a sight. Being that the Philippines is steeped in Catholicism, I was quick on my feet and said, "Don't worry, this is not the Stigmata." Their shock and horror quickly turned to laughter. I think many of them truly thought that it was a sign from God. It was really funny. Shirley and I still laugh about it to this day.

I wish I had ministered more in the Philippines. But that just wasn't the mission, I suppose. It seemed that my Father wanted me and my beautiful bride to honeymoon. Soon we would be going through many trials together. In hindsight, I'm glad that the Lord did this. Historically, it's been hard for me to rest. The Lord practically has to force me.

After that fast and the preaching, Nathan, Jordan, Shirley and I all decided that it was God's will for them to come with us to China. God had given Jordan some pretty awesome dreams confirming the whole thing. After three or four weeks in the Philippines we became a ministry team and we were off to our next destination, together.

I was so happy to have people of faith traveling with us. Nathan and Jordan were just wonderful. We were a pretty awesome team!

Δ   Ω

The Lord led us to Hong Kong to get our visas. It was very clear that we were to enter China through Hong Kong. We arrived in Hong Kong knowing no one and having no plan but to follow the leading of the Lord. We waited at the airport for direction, but it seemed God was being quiet. It was getting later and later, so I was sort of pushing us along. Finally, I found a map, and on it I saw a region called, *Jordan District*. Being that Jordan was with us, I said, "Hey let's go there!" Everyone agreed since we didn't have a whole lot of other direction. And suddenly we were on our way.

We arrived in the Jordan District and walked around to try to listen to the leading of the Lord. The morale of our women was plummeting because we were lugging around so much luggage and it was quickly getting late. I guess it was 9:30 when we arrived at Jordan District. Nathan and I kept praying and trying to keep the girls full of faith. But it was more than obvious that the joy and excitement was quickly departing.

After what seemed like hours wandering around trying to find God in Hong Kong, we went through a certain alleyway and up a narrow set of stairs . . . suddenly, there was our miracle. We had randomly arrived at the intersection of Nathan and Jordan Road! That's right! In the middle of Hong Kong we randomly found Nathan and Jordan Road!? We didn't have GPS. It was the sign we needed that we were on the right path. We were all overjoyed. It may seem like a small thing, but when you are simple children of God, trying to obey His voice with everything inside of you, it sometimes gets hard. Then when God suddenly shows up, when he suddenly reminds you that He truly will never leave you nor forsake you, you instantly return to peace, remembering, "God loves me!" I am sure we shed a few tears of joy as we stood there staring at that intersection.

Shirley and Jordan really needed that very literal sign. I think maybe Nathan too. I am sure Nathan and Jordan were wondering if they had made a big mistake in coming. I too was wondering that a little bit; I did not want to mislead my young brother and his precious wife, my little sister in Christ. I loved them very much and I wanted them to see with all my heart, *the power of God*. We all stood there and marveled at the seemingly impossible odds of finding a *Nathan* and a *Jordan Road* intersecting anywhere in the whole world, let alone in Asia! After that it was easier to trust that God is with us!

We ended up just getting a hotel room for the evening and ordering in food. But our money was quickly running out. So we were going to need another miracle of provision.

Δ   Ω

I guess I should explain here that early on in my learning to walk with God, I realized that I couldn't ever ask for money. I realized that if I was to make my needs known I might be working against the hand of God, tugging on people's heart strings. So I learned to be very quiet about any issues of provision. I have seen over and again, that God comes through, every time. Sometimes He comes through at the very last minute, but it's not the last minute to Him; it's perfect timing.

Our money was almost gone. We had been in Hong Kong for a few days and now we would have nowhere to stay that night. The girls were less than comfortable to say the least when we woke up that morning. But I was proud to see them both trying to use their faith with everything inside of them. Nathan was quiet, trying to hear the Lord's voice, and praying often. I was watching everything going on, watching for the leading of the Lord as we went throughout the city, seeking where God would have us to be and minister.

We came to a crowded bridge above a busy street when a certain woman, with a cross around her neck, walked by and Jordan said, "I have to talk to her." Jordan spoke with the woman and she mentioned a good church she knew of that we could attend. She told us how to get there and we all decided that it was the Lord. Our hopes were high, but when we got to the church it was closed. We stood outside trying not to lose heart, but it was a struggle for all of us to stay hopeful. Hong Kong was a difficult place spiritually. We all felt the spiritual oppression of that city.

Just as we stood there quietly wondering what we should do next, a man came and opened up the church. He was one of their pastors. We explained to him how the Lord had led us to Hong Kong and then to his church, and he directed us to go to the church offices. By the end of the day, I had a preaching gig and we had a place provided for us to stay! Shirley was especially happy because we would be housed by Christian Indonesians, and just like that our Hong Kong ministry was up and running! It was a great miracle. But we would need another great miracle very soon.

We got to the Chinese Immigration Office and were told, "No. You may not enter China." Talk about a big blow to our hopes and plans, the immigration officer wanted Shirley to return to her country, get a visa there, and then they would let her enter China. My wife was so adorable. She said, "I will go back to Indonesia and you all can go on without me. Robert, you can come and get me afterwards…" *No way*, I thought, *I'm not leaving my wife!* I sat there and prayed about what to do. I assured Shirley that God wasn't asking us to separate just a couple months after we married.

Trying to keep hope alive, I went back to the immigration window and asked to speak with someone who was in charge. A few moments later a very stoic and somber looking fellow nearly my height, pretty tall for an Asian man, came to the window to speak with me. He explained how there was *no way* that they were going to give us my wife's visa, he said, matter of fact, "There is no way I am going to let her into China. She has to return to Indonesia first."

It was like something out of Star Wars, I used the "Jedi mind trick". I said, "Sir, I am going to need you to reconsider. We cannot return to Indonesia. I need you to give us the visas." And I looked him straight into the eyes as I pushed our passports back thru the window to him. I couldn't believe it! He said, "Fine, give me three days and if everything checks out okay I will give you the visas." He took our passports and three days later we went and got our visas! God had done another miracle. It was awesome; I had never done the Jedi mind trick before!

Δ   Ω

One of Jordan's dreams came completely true in China. Jordan had a dream that both she and Shirley would be pregnant within two weeks of each other. Well, that would truly be a miracle because before Shirley and I married, Shirley told me, "Robert, you need to know before we get married that I cannot have children. I had an accident as a child and three or four doctors have told me that I will never be able to have kids." I responded to her, "Honey, God put us together. I trust Him. If He wants us to have kids He can grow you brand new ovaries or give us a baby in any way He sees fit."

I of course wanted children. I love big families. My dad adopted a total of ten and my mom birthed six, or seven, including a still-born, so I had long believed that I would have a big family. When Shirley told me this I was bummed for only a moment, then I chose faith, "God will provide." I told her. Then... in China it happened!

As Jordan's dream went, Jordan was the first to get pregnant and then two weeks later, practically to the day, my Shirley was pregnant; the best miracle of my life! My wife was going to have a baby. I was beyond excited! I wondered what the Lord would have me to do. I prayed but I didn't hear the Lord telling me to stop the mission, so we continued.

But I did feel badly for the girls as we kept traveling, almost the whole time we were in China. The Lord gave us specific instructions about where to go and what to do. We were on trains about half the time we were in China. Our pregnant wives were on trains; smelly, loud, uncomfortable trains with holes in the bathroom floors for toilets. Imagine those horrible conditions for their first weeks of pregnancy. Often, sometimes daily, I felt like the worst husband ever, but the Lord kept reassuring me that He was with us. I continued to pray, wondering if the Lord would change His mind.

We were not expecting to stop our journey in China. One day while preaching in Indonesia a woman stood up and said, "I saw a vision of you preaching in Russia!" I was preaching on an Island, a two-hour flight from Jakarta when that woman had that vision. Then on the flight back to Jakarta I *just so happened* to sit next to the only Russian missionary to ever come to Indonesia. We spoke about this miracle for nearly an hour before the flight landed in Jakarta. God confirmed beyond the shadow of a doubt that He was sending me to Russia; within 24 hours of this woman telling me, "God is sending you to Russia" I met the only Russian missionary to ever come to Indonesia, and he was seated right next to me on the flight! Try to figure out those odds.

Nathan and Jordan were really thinking that God wanted them to come to China and Russia with us, but Jordan's morning sickness was getting worse. Then Nathan got a horrible rash on his inner thighs and high fever. We were in this small town, in interior China. I felt horrible for Nathan. The rash got so bad he could hardly walk. So between the morning sickness of our wives and Nathans rash and fever, we were struggling pretty hard when we were ministering in that small town.

Then to make matters worse, somehow we ended up on the Chinese government's radar. One day I was approached by a man in the marketplace. He looked rather soldierly, and asked to see my passport and visa. My interpreter explained to me that he was an undercover policeman. His superior officer showed up within minutes and we were taken back to the church where we were being housed. Something like eight or ten cops were at the church waiting for us when we arrived. I saw looks of horror on the face of my wife and the pastor. I felt my stomach sink to my toes as I started to pray.

Nathan did not leave his room because he was so sick and Jordan stayed with him to take care of him, even though she was struggling with morning sickness. I asked Shirley to go and spend time with them while I spoke with the police. They questioned me for something like an hour. By my interpreter's body language and the nervousness of the pastor, it seemed I was going to jail. The officer in charge did not seem to believe my story about why we were in his small town. I told him that we were tourists. He said that he was going to take all of us into custody to be interrogated.

I pleaded with him to take me, but to leave everyone else at the church. I promised them that they wouldn't go anywhere while I was in custody. The officer was not happy and getting irritated for some reason. This tension built for the next forty or so minutes while I tried to say only exactly what the Lord told me to say. The moment came when I was certain he was standing up to put handcuffs on me, but then for no apparent reason at all, he started smiling. He stuck out his hand and said, "Welcome to China!" in broken English. He turned, spoke to the other officers and left. The majority of the police left the church with him. A couple of them stayed behind to try to practice English with me, it was as if I was now of celebrity status.

What did God do? In a moment we went from being arrested to being *welcomed* to China! The remaining officers stayed with us in the church and asked me questions about my life and America, while my translator helped us communicate. Everyone was very happy to be getting to know me. Then finally, the remaining officers left with great joy and appreciation. I wonder to this day what God did. I am sure I will find out in heaven. God is so awesome!

Again I could write books about all these things that happened on the road. But the other fun story I wanted to share while in China, was the day I went on a walk with the town's English teacher. His English wasn't great, but it was good enough for us to have simple conversation. As we were discussing the Chinese language I bent down and wrote a symbol in the dirt that I saw in my head. He was shocked. He said, "Do you know what you just wrote?!" I said, "No. I just saw this symbol in my head." He said, "That is the Chinese Character for *heaven*. You just wrote heaven on earth!" We laughed at how amazing that was and continued our talk and hike up the mountain.

We left that small town shortly after nearly being arrested and ended up in Beijing preparing to go to Russia, but Nathan's rash was getting worse and Jordan's morning sickness wasn't improving at all. It was very hard to think of our friends leaving, but it had become clear that it was time for them to go home to California. I will never forget that hectic day in Beijing as we bought train tickets to go north and they bought flights home. I had rarely ever had a friend like Nathan, with the guts to believe God with me, in those extreme ways. I didn't want to let him go, but I knew it was time.

Nathan and Jordan left the train station for the airport and Shirley and I got on a train headed for the northern-most border into Russia. It was a very sad train ride for us. We hardly talked at all for nearly twenty hours. Shirley loved to have the company and friendship of Jordan, and Nathan was more than a brother to me. Shirley and I hardly talked for the next day or two we were so bummed. But we had to get to the border immediately because our visas were expiring. On that train ride Shirley started to get really sick from her pregnancy. It was a very very difficult week after Nathan and Jordan left.

But God continued to give us grace.

Chapter 16

God gave Shirley an awesome dream in China. She was really suffering when an angel came to her in a dream. She said, "He was very tall and looked sort of Chinese, but taller than a normal human. We were in a café. He came and sat down next to me and you although you couldn't see him. He told me, "Don't worry. You are in the wilderness and it will be difficult. But God will get you through this." I didn't say much in response. Then the angel got up and went over to a window and sort of floated out into the air." Shirley needed this dream to get her through many of the tough times that would lie ahead for us.

When we finally made it to that Northern Chinese border, our visas were ready to expire that day. We had to leave China immediately. We got off the train and jumped into a taxi and headed for the border crossing. At the border crossing we learned that they would not, in any way, issue us Russian Visas at the border. (Yes, I tried the Jedi mind trick again, but it didn't work this time.)

I had to take the risk and go to the border hoping to get visas there. Our visas were expiring and I had to leave China, I had no option. Now I was in a small town far away from any Embassy in Northern-most China, with my pregnant wife with very little money. Our visas would expire by the end of the day, what would I do?

It's a very long story, but we finally found the right person to help us, and by the end of the day we had spent the last of our money on two-day visas and train tickets back to Beijing. They would only give us a two-day extension on our visas because we weren't near any place where they issue visas. We had to go immediately to the Russian Embassy to apply for our visas which was in one of two cities, Beijing or Shenyang. We bought our train tickets to head to Beijing, but while on the train I thought I heard the Lord, so I changed my mind and we got off the train in Shenyang. Of course we knew no one in the city.

We had enough money left for food and a night in a hotel. We went to the hotel and ate a good meal and rested the night. I prayed asking God would He was going to do to get us out of this trouble. He seemed to be awfully quiet. Shirley was her sickest as we stayed in that hotel, throwing up regularly and very unhappy with me.

I woke up the next morning and prayed; I really felt peace. I just knew that God was definitely going to come through for us. Shirley was miserable and very worried about what would become of us in China. She was especially concerned that we would get arrested for letting out Visa's expire. I assured her, God would come through. "He will save us, again." I told her. I left the hotel room with little plan of where to go but with lots of faith. I just knew that God was going to lead me somewhere. I didn't always have this surety of hope but I did that morning.

In the hotel lobby I noticed a prostitute sitting by herself, seemingly out of place. I saw a tattoo on her right shoulder; it was a Bible Scripture in English!? The tattoo said, "Trust in the Lord with all your heart and do not lean on your own understanding, in all your ways acknowledge Him and He shall direct your paths." That was truly the message I needed that morning. I decided to talk to her.

I sat down next to the prostitute and asked her about the tattoo. She spoke perfect English, without an accent even! We talked for quite a while, she told me how she had been a Christian all her life and was raised in a Christian home in China. She had come to America for school and while she was at a University in the south she lost her relationship with God. When she came home to China, her father had passed away, rather young, and she lost her faith completely. She was very ashamed to be sitting next to me. I could tell. I assured her that she had no reason to feel uncomfortable that I too was a great sinner saved by grace. She started to weep as I talked about God's love for us.

She changed the subject after wiping the tears from her eyes, "I can't do this right now," she said. "I have to work." I was very sad for her. She felt like my little sister. I was really sad, thinking about what she might do the rest of that day. Before leaving, she asked me a few questions and I ended up telling her quickly about our difficult visa situation and all the problems we had had the past few days. She said that she would call a pastor who knew her father very well and that he would probably be able to help us. She told me to wait for her call in our hotel room. She said that she would call by 10 am.

I went upstairs and told my wife all the good news. It was 8:30 am or so. We waited watching the phone. 10 am, 11 am and then finally close to noon the phone rang. It was her. As it turned out, that pastor friend of her father's had just been released from a 3-year jail sentence for propagating the gospel outside of the approved government churches; working in the underground church. She told me that he would put us in danger if he was to help us and that we should go and talk with someone else. She gave us the information on another pastor not far from our hotel. And she assured me that he would help us.

It a long story, but by the end of the day we had our visas. And we had two new best friends, Teacher Quan from China, and Pastor Emmanuel from Africa. The Lord suddenly grafted us into a whole new family of people, and we received a two-week extension on our visas. We were able to minister again and share the word of the Lord. I preached at Pastor Emmanuel's church and often shared with Teacher Quan. The book of revelation is illegal in the Chinese government churches, so a lot of our conversation centered around *last days prophesy* and end times events. It seemed to be news to Teacher Quan that so many *last day's events* were unfolding all across the world. We had a wonderful time sharing. And Shirley was happy again. She saw God's love for us again, and her hope was restored.

We were still unable to get our visas into Russia while in Shenyang, so the Lord directed us back to Hong Kong. At the Russian embassy in Hong Kong we were finally able to get our visas. We rested at a guest house on an island outside of Hong Kong. It was a great time of refreshing and even some fun. I started to teach Shirley to swim while we were there. It was the down time we really needed. God had provided for us tremendously, then, finally we got our Russian Visas! It was another 30-hour-plus train ride and a second 12-hour train ride to the border but we were finally at our destination.

My precious wife was terribly sick as we arrived to Russia.

Δ   Ω

The train arrived early in the morning. The night before, the train conductor had mercy on us and moved us into a room on the train with comfortable beds. We slept the whole night. I came to really love those Chinese people. When we got to that border town the fog had moved in and it was very cold. We didn't have many warm clothes having come from Indonesia, Philippines and Hong Kong in the summer time. It was the beginning of September and the cold came early to Russia that far north and east.

Shirley got off the train and was upset to say the least. She threw up a few times and was shivering with the cold. I remember that day clearly, because she had never seen her breath before in the cold air. It was all upsetting to her. I thought it was kinda cute that she had never seen her breath before but I had to keep all my smiles inside because she was feeling so terribly. I prayed and prayed that God would show up with great power to deliver Shirley from her suffering.

The Russian border was a total mess with people pushing and shoving, and my little 110 pound, 5' 3" pregnant-wife in the middle of it all. I grabbed a Russian soldier and explained to him using hand signals that Shirley was pregnant. Praise God. He ushered us right to the front of the line. And only moments later, we were in Russia! After all that trouble, all those trains and visa complications, sickness and struggle, we were finally there. As usual we knew not one person in Russia.

So we were nearly broke, again. We knew no one and did not speak a word of Russian. (Well, I knew, *Dasvidaniya*. Which means of course, *Goodbye* but that's it.) Shirley was doing her best not to completely loose it on me. She was so unhappy, my poor beautiful wife. I reminded her of her dream in China when the angel came to her and comforted her and told her that God was going to get her thru all of this, but she didn't seem to be very comforted by hearing about the dream. She just wanted to stop feeling sick. There was nothing I could do. I felt so helpless. I needed God to show up immediately.

I prayed and the only thing that came to me was, go to the church. We found a taxi and the woman taxi-cab driver called her daughter who spoke some English. I explained to her that I wanted to go to the "Protestant" Church. She seemed to understand but her mom took us to the Orthodox Church instead. Then it seemed like she overcharged us? Shirley was so angry at her. I told Shirley not to worry about it. We got out of the car and went inside of the Russian Orthodox Church.

Shirley said, "You told her to take us to the Protestant Church. How do you know that God is with us?" I told Shirley, "I don't know, maybe He is, maybe He isn't, but here we are. Let's see what happens. I don't feel like God is telling us to leave." Shirley was not convinced, so she went sulking off into the corner to try to get warm. I stood nearby the entrance of the old Church praying. After a few moments a man outside motioned to me, we could not communicate, but he seemed to be telling me that he was going to get someone. I waited just outside to see what would happen.

After twenty minutes or so a tall, authoritative, well-groomed looking man with a black robe down to the floor and a rather long beard, approached me. He spoke broken English but enough to understand that I was a minister of God. He said, "I know someone for you to talk to." I told Shirley the good news, but she was unimpressed. After another hour, a young man, seven or so years younger than me, showed up, His name was (is) Gregory.

He spoke nearly perfect English. He was one of the main English teachers at the high school. He asked me many questions, and I told him how God had miraculously sent us to his town. I told him about a dream God had given me in China, directing me specifically to his small city, and also about all our complications getting to him that day. He invited us to his home, "Let's go eat and figure out what God is doing." I was smiling like a little child, so happy that we were with this obvious brother in the Lord. Shirley was starting to have hope. She wasn't smiling but she wasn't as upset anymore either.

On the way to his home Gregory asked me if I knew how to make lasagna. I laughed at his odd request and said, "Well, it just so happens that my mother is Italian and I grew up cooking. I actually can make a pretty good lasagna." He was happy to purchase all the ingredients and we went to his home and started to cook lunch. He was very kind, very direct and clearly of a different culture than Indonesia or America, but he was also kind and sincere. I liked Gregory from the moment I met him.

We were at his home for nearly two hours having only small talk. To me this was quite strange because of all the events that brought us to his home. But I continued to be patient and let him talk about whatever he was interested in. Finally, in the midst of all this light-hearted conversation, Gregory said, "Do you want to know why I know that it is the Lord who brought you to my home!?" I was on the edge of my seat, "Yes! Tell me, please."

Gregory went on to explain to us that his seven-month old son was very sick and close to death in the hospital. He explained that he hadn't slept for the past three nights because he was up and praying that God would do a miracle for his son. He said, "And then, out of nowhere, you two show up and say, God sent you to my town." He continued, "I believe God sent you to me because He heard me praying and I believe that you are going to pray for my son and God is going to heal him." I was beyond overjoyed by what God had done. Shirley was in shock, but overjoyed too. We were more than ready to pray for Gregory's son.

It was only a simple prayer but I felt God heard us, and that the boy was healed. Later that day we got word from Gregory's wife, the boy had finally stopped throwing up, and his fever was down. He never threw up again. God healed him immediately! And Sasha is alive and well to this day! God saved Gregory's boy, his Sasha! This God, our Father, He really loves us. He loves American's, Indonesian's, Chinese, and He loves the Russians. Gregory would not let us leave his home for a few days. But then he found us a better place to stay, a place that would be more comfortable for my pregnant wife.

We met our dearest Olga and Andre next. We were hosted by these precious people with their daughter Sasha and Jackie, the dog. We were with that family the rest of our time in the Russian Far East. I was able to preach a few times at Baptist churches and we were really enjoying getting to know Russia. Olga treated us like gold and we left their lovely little town with tears and great sorrow. But it was time for us to go to Moscow, as the Lord was leading. We would greatly miss our Russian friends.

$$\Delta \quad \Omega$$

It was a six-day train ride across the whole country before we arrived in Moscow. Honestly I wish we had never gone to Moscow. It seemed like every Christian we met was cold, calloused and angry. Even the American missionaries we met in Moscow were unloving and harsh. God had given me a series of dreams about America, but we had our sights set on going to Germany. I wanted to meet back up again with Matthias, my German friend that I met in Israel, but the Lord kept closing the doors. It was clear, we were going to return to the U.S.

One day in Moscow the Lord directed us to a certain church to the north of the city. The pastor we met turned out to be the head of a denomination. God gave me a very clear word for him, a *word of knowledge*. When we got to his church, he became very upset with me and started to ridicule me for traveling with my pregnant wife. He hated the word from the Lord I gave him and he continued to ridicule me in front of my wife. Saying to me, "No man of God would drag his pregnant wife around the world with him! You think you are serving God but you are not. You need to return to your country and rethink what you are doing." When my wife started to cry I got very angry! "What happened to you?" I said. "You used to love Jesus and serve Him with all your heart. But now you are just another religious ruler, incapable of loving those God sends to you!" I said other things that seemed to break through the hardness of his heart.

But nothing I could say could get him to receive us or the message that God had given me for his church, "I won't let you preach that message," he said. "You are never going to preach at my church. And that's final. But I will help you." I tried to calm my emotions down as he tried to love us as best he was capable of. It was a very upsetting encounter. Then that pastor explained to us that a group from Peru had just come to him with almost the same message that I had just given him. He told us how they showed up out of nowhere and spoke very similar words to him. But still he wouldn't receive us, and still wouldn't receive our message. It was a very sad day in the kingdom of God.

The right hand man of that pastor gave us a ride back to the city and tried to explain to us why he thought that God had sent us to them. He explained how zealous for God that pastor used to be, but now with all the responsibilities of running over forty churches, he had lost something. I said, "If you speak with the tongues of men and angels and understand all kinds of prophesy but have not love. What does it profit you?" It was a very sad time in Moscow. The only people who received us the whole time we were there were the unchurched people. We ministered as much as we could.

And then suddenly it was all over. Our 30-day visas expired and we were on a flight headed back to Indonesia to get Shirley's visa things together and then on to America. It would take some months to prepare all the paperwork so we would minister in

Indonesia again but now as a married couple. I was happy to be returning to our friends and family in Indonesia. I was especially happy for Shirley. She would be very comforted being back with her family and friends. She would be fussed over and celebrated. I was happy for her and our little baby in her belly!

After practically 24 hours of flights and layovers, we arrived in Jakarta.

And the suffering was over. At least for a while . . .

Chapter 17

Again, I would not encourage anyone to get married after a month knowing each other and immediately take his bride out on the mission field for their honeymoon. That first year of marriage was very tough for us. I often thought of myself as a very loving person, full of the love of God, but after Shirley and I were married I realized I had really been kidding myself. I was broken and fleshly just like everyone else. Marriage became the mirror that I needed to see myself more clearly.

I wanted to love Shirley perfectly, but so many things got in the way. More than anything else it was *fear*: the fear of her leaving me, the fear of divorce, the fear of a horrible marriage for the rest of our lives, etc. Those fears and more kept me from having my heart open and willing to love her no matter the circumstances. Maybe I wasn't the worst husband ever, but I certainly wasn't the best.

I'd had a dream that I thought would come true in China because one of the main characters was a Chinese woman but it never did. So back in Indonesia, one day I was asked to go and pray for a couple that was barely still married. They fought terribly for days on end. My dearest friend, Edy the pastor, asked me to go and pray with them. Sitting there talking with them I was reminded of that dream I'd had months earlier. The man's wife was of Chinese decent.

The dream basically was: *We were in a room with hardwood floors. There were others in the room, but the one who I could see clearly was this Chinese woman. I was praying for her and as some spirit left her the whole house shook with a great earthquake!* It was a very real dream I still remember it to this day.

Suddenly sitting in front of this Indonesian man with his Chinese wife I was reminded of the dream. I asked them, "Do you have a room upstairs that has hardwood floors?" The whole downstairs of the house was tiled and hardwood floors are not common in Indonesia, so I thought that it was a long shot. But then they looked at each other and said, "How do you know that?" I told them about my dream and you could feel the level of expectation rise in the room as we all wondered what God was about to do.

Edy started to play the guitar when we got into the *upper room* and everyone joined in singing praise songs to God. The Holy Spirit showed up and the man whose marriage was having such troubles started to weep. As the power of God showed up I was the next one weeping. I started to think about my marriage and how odd it felt to be praying for this man's marriage when I was doing such a mediocre job at mine. I started to pray that God would make me more loving and take away my fears of opening up my heart to my wife. I wept greatly as I prayed aloud.

As I prayed, Shirley started to weep very hard also and Edy too. It had been a tough start to our marriage and I am sure Shirley was hoping that part was finally over. Finally, every eye in the room, except for that Chinese wife, was full of tears as the Holy Spirit continued to minister to us. Edy sang praise songs and we continued to pray. It was time for me to go and pray for the Chinese wife. She was very stoic and closed off as I approached her. I could feel years of bitterness, disappointment and pain as I prayed for her. I don't remember what I said, but as I prayed the power of God overwhelmed her until she wept the loudest and heaviest of us all. God was healing her. He was healing us all.

There was a great spiritual earthquake as I prayed for her! The whole dream had come true! It was another tremendous miracle. Last I heard, that couple is still married to this day, and doing better than ever. God is so good. He does miracles even to save marriages. What can't this God do? I am so very impressed with His closeness and His intimate love for each of us. I remain in awe of Him.

Δ   Ω

Those five months in Indonesia went by rather quickly. We went to the island where Shirley was born and I met all her extended family. (I met her mother's family. I never did meet her dad or any of his family.) We returned to Jakarta and I preached all over the island of Java. I preached at a prison, I preached at the Indonesian police academy: I must have preached fifty times during those five months in Indonesia. I was even able to disciple some young men of God. It was a great time of rest and reward watching God do many amazing things.

One time we went to pray for an older man, who had just had a massive heart attack, the whole left side of his body was paralyzed. He couldn't even open his left eye when we got to the hospital. As we were praying for him he opened his left eye. As the story goes, this man was released from the hospital a couple days later with 100 percent recovery. They had told him he would never use the left side of his body again, but that was before Jesus healed him.

We saw demons cast out, many words of prophecy come true, and words of knowledge spoken. A few other people we prayed for didn't seem to get healed. Shirley inquired about this, "Why when we prayed for the man with a heart attack did God heal him, but when we prayed for the sick man, he died?" I responded, "Jesus does the miracles, honey. We just believe in His Word and He does the rest. I don't know why He didn't heal that man?"

It was nearing the time for me to go back to the U.S. The process with Shirley's visa was taking longer than I had expected, and I would need to hurry it up if we were going to make it back to the U.S. to have the baby. It was a very hard decision, but it seemed like the Lord was leading me to leave my pregnant wife in Indonesia as I went ahead to America to work on getting her visa.

I could hardly say goodbye to Shirley at the airport I was so full of emotions. It was one of the hardest things I have ever had to do, leaving Shirley six months pregnant in Indonesia. I told her not to cry. I didn't want to see her cry. It was already too hard just leaving. I choked back tears so that she wouldn't get too emotional. My heart was so afraid. I hoped I was making the right decision. I prayed, "Lord, I really need a sign right now. I need to know that I am in fact making the right decision."

As I came to the terminal I saw someone I knew, Samuel another pastor. The last time I had seen him we prayed, "If its God will that we should reunite He will miraculously connect us again." So we specifically did not exchange contact information. It turned out that he was on the flight with me! I had a layover in Taiwan and he was going there to interview about taking over a church. I ended up leaving the airport with him in Taiwan, and going to meet some of his friends during my ten-hour layover. It was a wonderful time. I got to share some of what God had been doing those years and to bless a pastor and his wife with words of encouragement. It was the miracle I needed to know the Lord was with me! Samuel and I are close friends to this day.

I flew to LAX with much more peace, even with all the turbulence, I had the sign from God that I needed. I hadn't seen Samuel since my first trip to Indonesia some seven months earlier. It was a great miracle to be on that flight with him. I had a long thirteen hours to think about all the things that the Lord had done as I was nearly back to the U.S. after almost three years being away. I was married! I would be a father soon! I had seen the Lord move for years like something you would read out of the book of Acts. But in a few hours I would be back in L.A., seeing friends and family and people I thought I might never see again.

It was a strange flight to say the least. I couldn't talk to anyone. I was sort of in shock.

Δ Ω

My arrival at the airport signaled that this would not be the easiest homecoming. My brother and his son were the only ones to greet me at the airport. Not one other friend or family member thought to come and welcome me home. I had been gone for three years and I would quickly learn that nothing had changed for the better in America in my absence. Often upon my return I felt like a Vietnam vet who had returned from a war and fought to make his country proud, but no one cared. Maybe no one wanted me to go and fight in the first place?

My family was very slow in welcoming me back into their hearts. It was a strange time. Only my sisters lovingly, received me home. Rebekah in fact had given her life to the Lord while I was gone, and she wanted me to know about it. One day I was preaching in California, at Nathan's family Home Church, and the Lord told me that there were people in the room who needed to be baptized. I asked the question and Rebekah started to weep. She said, "I refused to be baptized until you came home. I told the Lord that I wanted you to baptize me. So I have been waiting for you . . . "

It was nearly 10:00 p.m. on a weeknight when we arrived at the beach to baptize everyone. There were a few others who wanted in on the baptism party with Rebekah. It was a cool winter night and the water would surely be freezing, but I rushed in ahead of everyone anyways. As I got into the water I lifted my hands and said, "Let the heavens witness the glory of the Lord!" I turned and saw that everyone had this look of awe on their faces. It turned out that as I proclaimed that the heavens would witness God's glory, a huge and very brilliant shooting star rocketed exactly behind my head. The heavens were in fact witnessing God's glory. I will never forget Rebekah's baptism. Then Nathan's brother had this awesome vision of me with Jesus. It was truly a night to be remembered!

I was immediately ministering again. Once while I was staying back in L.A., visiting some friends, a new brother named Rob and his family, I was praying for this girl who was deeply involved in witchcraft for many years. She told us about how she had invited demons to come live inside of her. At the time she didn't understand that they were demons, she called them *spirits* and these spirits took over her mind and body. She was in Texas when she asked the demons to come live inside of her. She didn't remember anything of what had happened to her for the next month, but when she was conscience again she was completely naked in Albuquerque, New Mexico walking down the side of a road as the authorities came and picked her up and took her to a mental hospital.

I met her while at Rob's house a few years after she had lost her mind and asked all those demons to come and live inside of her. (She told us how she could physically feel the demons crawling down into her stomach!?). She would say that she wanted to be set free of the demons but then she would act like she was against us. It was a very strange experience. She was dating one of Rob's friends in the church, a minister-type. It seemed to me that she was on an assignment to derail this man of God and it was working. We prayed for her through the night but she fought us, continually. In visions I saw something like thirty demons leave her, but the Lord told me that there were many more. He said, "This will help her to at least be able to see that I love her so she can receive me into her heart." Jesus would set her free at any point in time, if she would only cry out to Him. Trying to help her was as strange an experience as I had ever had before!

A month later, while preaching in a half-way house where all these guys were either just out of jail or just off of drugs, I had this revelation, "I am going to have a daughter and I am going to name her, Goodness." It was the strangest thing. It just hit me, like an epiphany. I stopped preaching and I told the guys in the room what the Lord had just showed me. I prayed in front of them, "Father confirm your word." Within a few minutes Shirley called me from Indonesia. I told her what had happened. She agreed to name the baby Goodness if it was a girl. Our ultrasounds were inconclusive. We still didn't know if we were having a baby boy or a girl.

God did so many miracles in getting Shirley back to me. She got her visa the last possible day she could have gotten it. I didn't have the money to buy her plane ticket until the day before she would be leaving! The Lord got her on a flight the last possible weekend that the doctors would allow her to fly. After 24 hours of travel, my poor pregnant wife flew into LAX. It was March 16th, almost two months to the day after I had left her in Jakarta.

By March 18th Shirley was having contractions and we went through three horrible days of trying to find the right place to have the baby. We wanted to have a home birth but the midwives were all busy (and I was broke.). The midwife we finally found ended up walking out on us at 12:30 in the morning of March 21st. It was clear to me that this baby was coming at any minute but the midwife was not convinced. At 1:00 a.m., just 30 minutes after the midwife left, Shirley's water broke! I wondered if I was going to have to deliver the baby myself. But Shirley assured me, "No way! Do you want me to die!? Just get me to the hospital!"

It was like a scene out of a movie. I rushed her to the hospital some fifteen minutes away. They met us at the entrance with a wheelchair. The doctor, whom everybody called Jim, not doctor but Jim, assured me that he could deliver the baby. He said, "It's been maybe twenty-five or thirty years since I have done this but it's like riding a bike, right?" It seemed like he was looking to me for reassurance, I said, "I have faith in you Doc. You are going to do a great job." I laughed because if I didn't laugh I was certainly going to flip out!

It was very comical, like having Robin Williams deliver our baby. "Jim" kept knocking things over in the delivery room and spilling his instruments all over on to the ground. When he knocked something over he would say, "Ooops. That's my fault. Sorry everyone." And then he would try to straighten his instruments up only to knock something over again. Then he would show me how to deliver the baby. He and I would sometimes end up talking and joking around so much that Shirley would have to yell at us, "Hey you guys! Another contraction is coming!" And then I would have to get serious and help her. All the laughter really helped me to calm down and enjoy myself. What made it even funnier is that "Jim" was not trying to be funny.

When the delivery began it was 2:00 a.m. exactly. Jim said, "Let's try to have this baby out by 2:30" to which I responded, "I like 2:22 better!" Jim agreed, "Okay, 2:22. Let's go team!" And Shirley started to push. Wouldn't you know it? Exactly 22 minutes later, my precious little girl . . . my Goodness from God came into the world to be with us! It was amazing!

You were so beautiful Goodie: hardly any blood on your body and you had the brightest most beautiful eyes! They almost didn't need to clean you off at all. Your mom was so tired she fell asleep and I held you. You looked me right in the eyes and I could tell that we were going to be close. You never cried when I held you. You were so tiny and precious. I loved you immediately, Goodness. And I will always love you.

After your mom, you are the best present God has ever given me!

Chapter 18

My life has not been without its share of grief and sorrow. It seems that in this world there is no escape from it. The pains of this fallen place will find us, one day or another. There is no amount of money, or family, or church, or spiritual fortitude that will hide us away from the certainty of suffering. The world is broken. We are not as close to God as we were intended to be and that is sad at times. Looking back, I have been grieving for the greater part of my life. But my marriage to Shirley was the dawning of the end of those, my years of sorrow.

It was hard not to be sad for Jesus' Church. He has such incredible things in store for us, but so many of us continue to settle for the crumbs off of the kings table. He has the most amazing *Thanksgiving Feast* imaginable, all laid out upon His table but we settle for so much less. The kingdom of God is ours for the taking but we settle for mere religion.

There is no avoiding it. This world is fallen. We were not made for this fallen place and so we must not hold on to it any longer. We must open up our hands and let God remove from them everything that offends, everything that holds us back and everything that is below the blessing He has in store for us. Only then, as empty vessels, can God fill us with His abundance. Once we are emptied out we can finally be filled with the fullness of the kingdom of God. *"Empty us out, Lord, so that only that which is of You might remain. Amen."*

One night while Shirley was fast asleep the sorrow was just more than I could bear! My family was being less than accepting of Shirley and my new little family, much of the church family throughout California was suffering and I felt very alone again.

I tried as best as I could to shake off those feelings of grief but everyday something upsetting was happening, again! I couldn't do it alone. I needed help! Help from heaven.

It was about 1 a.m. when I went out onto our balcony. We were staying in a friend's guest house out in the countryside. There were no lights at night so the stars and the view from our deck were incredible! As I sat outside looking into the beauty of the "Milky Way" (I could see it with my naked eyes!) I spoke with the Lord about my life. I told Him about all my woes and pains and I said, "Father I just need joy! Please Father. Give me and my family joy even in the midst of all this sorrow . . . "

The Lord responded as He often does with a question, "Did you know that that's the first time you have ever asked me for joy!?" *I wept at the thought of it. What was wrong with me*, I thought, *why have I never asked my Father for joy!?* The Lord interrupted my thoughts, saying, "You just don't know how much I love you." I fell to my knees and wept aloud. I thought about all the things that I never asked Him for: love, peace, contentment, strength, etc. It was overwhelming to think just how little I believed in my Father's love for me. With all the sincerity I could muster, I said, "Then Father, I am asking You now for joy!" Exactly as the word "joy" came out of my mouth I was quite startled when hundreds of birds flew out of the tree in front of me and up over my head, around and around several times. And then they flew back into the tree from where they had come.

God had heard me. The flock of birds over my head in the middle of the night was my witness. It was such an amazing thing to witness. *But why would God do such a miracle just for me? No one else is here to see it?* I thought. I heard Him repeat, "You just don't know how much I love you." I couldn't go back to sleep. I sat there through the night talking to Him about all kinds of things . . . It was absolutely one of the most special times I have ever had alone with my Father.

I was back in L.A. and I met up with the pastor I had given that warning to in 2010, wherein the Lord tried to get his attention so that he would stop commingling business and church affairs. I knew his life had gone downhill since I had last seen him, but I had no idea how badly. When he showed up to our meeting at Carl's Jr. he had a huge bandage on the side of his face. I learned that he had to wear it because of the surgery he had to remove the tumor from his brain. It was horrible. I was so broken hearted for my dear friend and elder in the Lord.

This pastor wasn't one of the bad guys. He was a hero who had gone astray. He worked with the least among us and served the brokenhearted, the poor, the forgotten ones and those who no one else wanted to deal with. He was a Christian Superhero in so many ways. He has books of stories in him, of all that he has seen God do over the years, but that wicked false prosperity gospel crept into his heart, unawares. It choked out the kingdom of God for a long season in His life. I had to choke back tears as we sat together, catching up and eating hamburgers near downtown Los Angeles.

He told me about all that had become of him while I was gone. He was broken but not destroyed, thankfully. This part of the conversation stood out to me the most. As I tried not to stare at the bandage on the side of his head, he said, "Maybe you can pray for me and help me to be restored." My response was, "Who am I to pray for you? You are my elder in the Lord." I thought for a moment and said, "I know several of your pastor friends. Let's go to them and talk with them about restoring you." He said, "Come on Robert, they don't care about me. You of all people should know that." I said, "What? What do you mean?" He said, "All these years of ministry and working alongside of so many of their ministries but they never cared about me. But I know that you care about me . . ."

I was beyond shocked to hear what the pastor was saying. If you knew this man you would love him as I loved him. He wasn't a terrible person. He wasn't "Bad". He was like us all, a sheep who had wandered astray and the pride of this life blinded him. I was leaving him feeling quite broken, but I knew for certain that the Lord would restore him. I don't know why I was so certain, there was no visible sign of things going good for him but I was sure of it nonetheless. He had repented and turned his heart back to God. I knew in my heart that he was very safe and he didn't need me at all. The Lord had heard all of his words and I wouldn't need to say or do anything. I thanked the Lord for letting me see how He had saved this pastor and his family. He should have died with a brain tumor that size and cancer so far along. It was a miracle that he was alive! It was a miracle that his wife didn't leave him with all the stuff that came out against him. God loves us all! The whole story is true!

The most recent news I have on him is that his ministry was rebuilt and is again thriving. Perhaps it isn't as big as it once was in numbers, perhaps he isn't hob-knobbing around with the whose-who of the church world in Los Angeles, but he is adding to the kingdom of God daily, still married to his wife and his children are helping to build the ministry. God saved him, totally!

Our God is so good. His mercy truly knows no bounds.

Δ   Ω

I had received a few dreams about Las Vegas those months after Goodness was born, so Shirley and I started to pray about going. It seemed that the Lord was sending us out again. One thing that the Lord was making very clear those months was that it was time to say Goodbye to California again for a while. I reconnected with many of my friends and family and what became abundantly clear to me was, that *a prophet truly is not without honor except within his own home, or country, or kindred.* It remains a very difficult task for the kingdom of God to thrive in a setting where people have known you since you were a child. I pray that the sons would remember this. It's nothing to be upset about, it's just one of the ways the kingdom of God works.

I was not thrilled about going to Vegas, remember that I was saved there, but I still didn't have many good memories of the place. But in one of the dreams I had, it seemed like we would be maybe starting a church, so I was at least excited about that possibility. Still I had no friends living in Vegas at the time, so we would be going totally by faith, again. A friend ended up paying for our rental car and we had four or five hundred dollars on us; we were rich by our usual travel standards! My wife, baby Goodness and I, were back on the road with Jesus.

Remember that Shirley was told that she couldn't have any children? Well only a couple months after Goodness was born, we were pregnant again! We were overwhelmed with joy! I think we were both very happy to be having another baby. I think Shirley was in shock for a few months but as the shock passed she was happy together with me. So I should say that I drove my newborn baby and my pregnant wife through the desert, onward to Vegas. I will never forget the conversation I had with my dad on the way, it was so anointed.

My dad called while we were on the highway and we must have talked for half the drive. God had given him a word for me, he said, "The Lord showed me that you are on your way out of the wilderness and into the Promised Land!" He said more, but this was what really stood out to me. It was the Lord. The Lord continued to confirm these words over the next several months. What the Lord was showing me was that The Promised Land is also a spiritual place, not just the Holy Land of Israel. It's the place where we come to trust God with our whole heart, and He takes us out of the wilderness and puts us into the land He has prepared for us. It could be a literal land, sure, but the point is that it is the Land of Promise: Life, and Life more Abundantly; the life Jesus promised to us. The Promised Land is that intimate and very personal place with our God, where we receive His Goodness and His Abundance! I was very happy for my wife; soon life wouldn't be so tumultuous and so bumpy.

Las Vegas was a miraculous time wherein many dreams came true and the power of God was revealed often. But in the end we had no open door to remain, no open door from the Lord to start a fellowship. I met with many new friends, new pastor friends and ministered to our host family often. We stayed with our new friends for a month or so and then we received marching orders for where we would go next. After a short time back in L.A., the Lord made it abundantly clear that we would not be returning any time soon, we flew to Detroit where we would spend the holidays with my dad and his family.

That trip to Detroit could not have gone any worse. Even though dad and I really seemed to be getting along, *a prophet is not without honor within his own home or with his own family.* We wanted to leave almost as soon as the plane landed. The intensity of the spiritual warfare was like nothing we had encountered in a long time. Everything was going wrong from the start. The enemy was working triple time to keep my dad and I divided. But Shirley and I were learning to be united in warring not against flesh and blood but against spiritual forces in high places set against us. Maybe going was a mistake? But the Bible says, "He works all things for good for those who love God and are the called according to His purpose."

Shirley was not raised believing in the baptism of the Holy Spirit. In fact, they taught her that speaking in tongues, among many of the other signs of the power of God, were no longer in existence. Now we had been married going on two years and she had lived to see that the power of God was indeed still alive and well. She was only just opening up to receiving the baptism of the Holy Spirit when we were in Detroit.

It was New Years and my dad wanted to *bring in the New Year* at a church service where there would be much prophesy and Spirit of the Living God. It was an awesome night. The praise and worship was incredible. The pastor opened the microphone and let me preach for fifteen minutes or so. The Holy Ghost was in full evidence that night. After the pastor's sermon, he had many of us from the congregation come up for prayer. He personally wanted to anoint Shirley, me and our baby, with oil.

My wife was five or six months pregnant at the time and showing a nice round baby-belly. As he laid his hands on Shirley, she collapsed to the ground. She had never experienced the Holy Ghost in such a way. In the past she had felt preachers push her over and practically force her to fall down. But this time, this pastor hardly touched her, it was the weighty glory of

God that overwhelmed her and buckled her knees, and sent her floating down onto the floor. It is an experience with God that she will never forget. She just never knew all this Holy Spirit stuff was real. She always thought that it was all a big show. Like I said, many a pastor tried to push her over. I was so happy to see my wife overcome with the reality of the presence of God. I had been praying for this since we met nearly two years before.

But all this time, even with the good things of God around us, I continued to grieve. The Lord assured me that my years of grieving were nearly over. One night in a dream or a vision, He came to me and said, "You are in the last stage of grieving. It will all be over soon." I had to look up what "the last stage of grieving" was. All the experts agreed that the final stage of grief is *acceptance*. What that meant to me was, "The Church is what it is, Robert. Now you will come to accept her and love her even in all of her brokenness. And loving her, you will be used to bring her closer to the Father . . . "

I held to these words with all my heart. Soon it would all be over. Soon we would be in the Promised Land and the grieving would finally end. Surely there would still be grief in this life, but the Lord had made it clear that I was in a process of grieving that was nearly over. It seemed that I was sharing in His grief those years. He was letting me see what He saw, even in part, and I was sharing with Him in that suffering. The Lord had shown me a lot, maybe almost too much for a young guy. But He was also faithful to take me through it and bring me out, new, on the other side.

I prayed diligently, believing that it was time to *cross the Jordan.*

Δ Ω

We left Detroit without tears, we were more than happy to be on our way. We had been led by the Lord to Arizona. I would be meeting up with a dear friend I hadn't seen since Bible College some fifteen years earlier. In Bible College days we were very close and intimate friends, but we had lost touch. It was Chip that I had started the door-to-door prayer ministry with; we were both very zealous for serving the Lord back then! After Bible College I had helped him a little in starting a church in Arizona, but we did not see eye to eye on everything so he continued on without me. These years later I found him to be offended, hurting, grieving, and having a hard time dealing with the church and the brokenness of the world, his suffering was much like mine had been.

It is hard to grieve with people around you. It's hard to share in each other's sorrow; look at Job and his friends. Suffering alone seems easier because you can hide away those feelings better, but when you have a friend to talk with, those hurts, anger and emotions come to the surface and without Christ, there can be terrible destruction. I have yet to find any other way for truly dealing with these kinds of deep and real hurts. There is only one way, as far as I am concerned; give them over to Jesus. Talk to your God! Tell Him, "Lord, it hurts. I'm tired of hurting. Take this away from me. Heal my broken heart. *Create in me a clean heart O God and renew a right spirit within me.* I can't do this alone. I need you Father!" Tell Him the truth. He will set you (us) free.

It was very slow going in Arizona with my long time friend and his family. We loved each other again from the start, but we were inching back towards walking with the Lord together. He told me years of stories, about all that he had seen in the church world, and how upsetting it all was for him. He told me about how his church ended up folding and the regrets associated with that time. My dearest friend was hurting so much and all I wanted to do was to make it stop. I could tell that his wife saw the same thing, but she also felt powerless in helping him. It was a hard trip; very hard on the heart.

I have not written to you every story of the brokenness of the church that I have experienced. Some are just too personal, and I have no desire to bad mouth God's holy church. I have not written about every pastor I have met, and the stories of their lives. But I have not told you a few of the stories of judgment falling on some of these religious and church leaders whom I have known. I have told you only a portion of just how broken God showed me that the church has been throughout this past generation. And none of this was His intention or idea . . .

But all of these things I had seen were definitely still with me. I was carrying them around like a huge weight, a heavy burden to be dragging behind. If you had told me that that's what I was doing I would have argued with you, for sure. I was burdened to say the least. I was so weighed down at that time in fact, that I could hardly pray anymore. Weeks would pass in California, Vegas, Detroit and then Arizona, that I was so tired and feeling weak that I couldn't even cry out to the Lord anymore. Had I seen too much? I didn't know what was the matter with me? I didn't seem depressed, but I was absolutely *not* happy. You have read the story; it was a lot for me to handle.

But my God was with me! He continued to give me strength and show me that He was nearby, even if I didn't pray or try to engage Him, He was engaging me. *He will never leave us, He will never forsake us.* Shirley was a huge help and Goodness too! They were a very comfortable and joyful place for me to rest in the Lord.

Just as the Lord never left my precious friend from Bible College, He would never leave me either. I think He had me go to Arizona for my friend and his family sure, but just as much for me and my family. I received much comfort being with my dear old friend and his family in Arizona. Sometimes when we are hurting we just need a safe place, a place where people aren't going to judge us or try to "fix" us but simply a safe place where we can rest for a while and let God back into our hearts, filling us afresh.

God permitted us to do one great miracle while in Arizona that trip. A friend of Chip's daughter's mother was having a baby and things went terribly wrong. The baby was born months premature and the mom was bleeding nonstop. They were very worried about losing both the mom and the baby. We were praying for them and somehow we decided that we had better to go to the hospital and lay hands on her and the baby.

It was evening when we arrived at the hospital. God stopped the mother's bleeding that day, so she was feeling full of faith and hope, she seemed to be full of faith and ready to have us lay hands on the baby. When we got to the baby's room the nurses seemed to be losing hope. Their faces were downcast and they explained that if the baby didn't improve immediately she probably wouldn't make it through the night. They would only allow me and Chip's wife to go in with the mother to pray for the baby.

All the baby's vital signs were extremely low. The feeling of despair was very thick in the room, but I started to pray anyway. I couldn't touch the baby inside of that incubator, but still the Holy Ghost showed up. It wasn't a long prayer or anything very eloquent, but as I started to pray we watched all the vital signs of the baby return to normal. The nurse's eyes grew big as he watched what the Lord was doing. The miracle happened right in front of our eyes!

The baby lived through the night and her vital signs remained normal every day thereafter. She was so little, around 2 pounds, so they kept her at the hospital for several more weeks until she was big enough to go home. She is alive and well to this day. It was another genuine Jesus miracle! We were all over-joyed to be a part of God's salvation plan for that family. This is one of my favorite miracles that God ever did! It was awesome to be with Chip and his family again, after all those years . . .

We were very clearly being sent to Hawaii next. So with much confirmation, dreams and miraculous signs of God we prepared to leave for the islands. We left Arizona and our dear friends with much sadness, but I also had tears of joy because I knew that the Lord had hold of my brother again and that he was going to be just fine. Soon he would be completely restored to the Lord, and his joy would return. It's hard, seeing so much of the brokenness of the Church, the Church that we love so dearly. But we don't change anything with anger, we don't fight fear with rage, we don't fight against pride with will-power, we fight against fear and all the iniquity of the world with the love of

God. God's love changes everything. It's always been His power, His Spirit, His love; making the changes. (Zechariah 4:6)

In Hawaii I had to receive a new measure of His love. There was no other option. Only God's love is going to change all that is broken. I was finally starting to see it clearly ...

We need more of Jesus! He is the answer ...

He has always been *The Answer*!

Chapter 19

Somehow it was hidden from me just how hurt and angry I was. My marriage helped me to see some of the other things in my heart. My dad too, he helped me to see myself better; to see the brokenness and the wounding still inside of me. One night Shirley had this dream, I was the Hulk. I wasn't an evil person or anything like that, in the dream I was even a super-hero. But I was the superhero who was known for turning into a giant rage-machine and destroying things. I totally understood what the Lord was speaking to me. It was a bitter pill and very hard to swallow but I got the message, loud and clear.

In Hawaii I started speaking to the Lord again . . . and often. I told Him about all that I had seen in His Church; the good, the bad and the ugly, as they say. I asked Him if there was anything I could do to be a part of helping to change things. But even more than that I asked Him to change me, I said, "I can't continue to serve You this messed up Lord. You have to make me a more loving person. Right now I am just upset too often. I get angry and frustrated too easily. I don't have enough love in me. I need more of Jesus!" The Lord told me, "Pray that I forgive your father." I couldn't see how praying for my dad would help me to not be angry anymore . . . How does this have anything to do with all of my problems and the problems of the church? But I obeyed the Lord anyway.

God gave me a good friend in Hawaii, his name was John. John and I would often meet up and pray, interceding not just for our dads but for the church "dads" at large; praying that God would forgive them. I had seen much of what they had done to injure the flock. I had seen more than enough to prove to me that we should "Call down fire" upon them! But my heart had changed along the way. I didn't want to call down fire anymore. I didn't want judgment anymore. I just wanted things to change. I just wanted things to be better. I didn't want that anyone would be destroyed.

I prayed that God would help the elders and church leaders to be less afraid. I prayed that God would give them courage and put His love in their hearts. John and I prayed and prayed, sometimes daily, and usually we prayed about the same issue, "God save our dads." John's dad was also a very religious man. John had seen more than his fair share of hypocrisy and brokenness in the church world. He had been involved with many very large church organizations and one that had fallen apart at its peak, due to the pastor's sexual immorality. John was another one grieving. God gave me a true brother to walk with for a time. John was really an intercessor!

It was ironic that I was praying this way so much in Hawaii, because at one point in time, a group of church "dads" seemed to band against me and resist the ministry of God in my life. I would often leave those Thursday morning prayer groups beaten up and troubled, but I would still go to the beach and pray for those men. The problem was so very clear and right in front of my eyes. God has to forgive these men, there is no other way. If He doesn't forgive them, what's to become of His Church? I prayed, fasted and prayed some more. "Father, forgive them for they know not what they are doing."

It was a great comfort and joy to be with John. There were others helping in this season of great breakthrough and anointing. But John was used by the hand of God more than anyone else in shouldering the burden with me. He remains a good brother in the Lord. And everyone needs good brothers in the Lord, even the pastors and the other church leaders, even the dads; everyone needs good brothers in the Lord.

Δ Ω

God did many new things with me in Hawaii. He gave me several new prophetic sermons to preach. I ended up preaching half a dozen times or so, throughout Hawaii. Then the Lord spoke very clearly to me, "Now it's time to start Discipling." About the same time He spoke that word to me, several young guys showed up out of nowhere. And the greatest miracle of all was that David *just so happened* to be living in Hawaii when God sent us there.

David is the youngest son of my dear friend Frank from California. David and I had known each other when he was a teenager, but I hadn't seen him in all these years. Now, in Hawaii, he was a young man of God, a praise and worship leader at a church plant and my new best friend. John was my big brother, he is older than me by six or seven years, and David was my little brother: almost young enough to be my son. These two men became my brothers-at-arms and together we fought spiritual battles, taking territory for God's Kingdom, on our way into *The Promised Land*.

The grieving was beginning to recede as I prayed for the forgiveness of The Church. New messages started to show up in my heart, I was often preaching about *Mercy, not Judgment*. I would say things like, "If everyone gets what they deserve, if it was an eye for an eye and a tooth for a tooth, we would all be blind and drinking from straws." Its mercy God wants: *mercy triumphs over judgment*. After all these years later, I was finally starting to understand the gospel.

John, David and I often cried out, "Mercy, Father! Have mercy on us! Have mercy on these men who have misled Your Church and injured Your Flock! Have Mercy, in Jesus name! Forgive the fathers!" Those early mornings on the beach were some of the most powerful prayer sessions I had ever had. I knew a breakthrough was coming. I knew that God was hearing us. I knew for sure that things were going to change. I was finally living out the gospel, praying for the salvation of the world. I was happy. I was a son of my Father. It's all that had I ever wanted.

One day I was ministering to a young man that had a certain problem with pornography. He was telling me with much shame about how bad his problem was, head hung low. When I looked at him I didn't see a disgusting porn addict, I saw a precious and innocent child of the Most High God, humbling himself and asking for help! I felt the Spirit come upon me and I said to him, "You aren't dirty! You aren't bad! You have a pure heart. And you know what the Bible says about the pure of heart? It says, Blessed are the pure of heart for they shall see God!" And exactly at the moment I said, "See God" an angel, like lightning appeared in the sky about fifty feet above the ocean! His countenance was so brilliant that it sent me back, falling against the rocks! My dear young friend started to weep without even knowing what had happened. It was one of the most amazing things I had ever seen!

I ministered daily in Hawaii as the Lord gave me grace but I also had a baby girl and a very pregnant wife! Shirley was getting so big she was about ready to pop! I was getting excited to meet the little guy. Every ultra-sound that we had told us that we were having a baby boy and we had everything together to welcome the little man into the world. We named him, "Noah Abel". The Lord even told Shirley the exact day that he would be born.

Sure enough, just as the Lord said, the morning of April 4th Shirley started having small contractions. This was such a peaceful labor compared with Goodness that I almost didn't believe that Shirley was really going into labor. About 2:00 in the afternoon the contractions were getting strong so we decided to head for the hospital. We grabbed our dear friend Pam. (Her hubby, Rafter, was going to meet us at the hospital. Pam and Rafter were Goodness' adopted grandparents. We met them on the island when we first arrived. They were our dear friends and our angels sent from heaven! We are close to them to this day.) Then the "birthing team" headed for the hospital.

The hospital was a one-hour drive away from where we were living, so Shirley was a little nervous that we wouldn't make it. I assured her that it would be fine. It was nearly 4:00 p.m. when we finally hit the road with Pam. Shirley was having contractions nonstop the whole drive north. We finally reached the hospital without any complications. Praise the Lord. It was so peaceful.

The nurses admitted us, but Shirley was hardly dilated at all. I assured them, "Don't worry. She will go from a 1 to a 10 in minutes." They decided to trust me. By 6:00 p.m. Shirley's water broke and we were delivering baby Noah! It was incredible. The nurses only let Shirley start pushing at 6:25 p.m. and at 6:36 our little baby was born! Only eleven minutes of pushing. What a blessing. What was even more incredible was that we had a *baby girl*!

I just kept staring at my new baby girl while she nursed, thinking, how did this happen? I kept wondering. It was so strange. How could everyone have been so wrong? Even my dreams? I had a very clear vision of my son. It was so unexpected. But she was God's gift to us, truly. I couldn't have been happier . . .

Honey, your mommy named you, "Mercy". You loved your mom from the start. You wouldn't come to me at all. You must have nursed for five hours straight! Your eyes were glued shut and your face was very puffy. You were much bigger than Goodness so your mommy was very sore after she pushed you out. Once the shock wore off about you not being a boy, I was very very happy that Goodness had a sister and we had our girlies. We couldn't have been any more content at the hospital that night, my precious daughter. You and your sister are God's greatest gift to me! You make me so happy . . . I know that God loves me every time I look at you, Mercy!

All of the sudden I had *Shirley, Goodness, and Mercy* who would be following me around all the days of my life." (Psalm 23:6) It's an incredible story. Maybe I wouldn't have believed it myself except that this is the life I have lived with The Lord.

All of this was more proof to me, as if I needed any more proof, that God in fact loves me. I have nothing to fear, ever, because God's love is true. He is faithful. He never lies, ever. He is better than we know. God's *Goodness* is past finding out and His *Mercy* knows no bounds!

And I had proof, one in my right arm and one in my left . . .

Δ Ω

Even with loads of adversity I was coming alive again in Hawaii. Many pastors withstood us and many of the elders wanted to unleash their judgments upon me, but God continued to give me the grace to forgive. Our life of faith was very offensive to several of them. The other men who seemed to like us didn't want to stand up to the rest of the group who would stand against us. But God continued to give me the grace to forgive. It would have been a much more difficult time but my beautiful wife and my two precious baby girls made me so happy every time I would come home to them. I would often come home irritated about the day's events, being rejected or worse, but with one look at my beautiful family I would melt like butter and my peace would return to me. God really knows what He is doing!

Shirley had a few new dreams. Instead of being the Hulk I had become *Superman!* God was changing me. I was starting to love again. The grief was departing and a new found joy was showing up. He was, in fact, turning my mourning into dancing and my weeping into joy. My Father was doing a brand new work in me and I was seeing Hope and Life again. I was beginning to see His power over the enemy, restoring all that was broken. It seemed that any day, Revival was going to break out. Life was really starting to get exciting in Hawaii!

One day I went over to my neighbor's house because they were dealing drugs out of that apartment and sometimes keep us awake until 3:00 or 4:00 in the morning. I decided to offer them Jesus instead of anger or judgment. They were very uncomfortable with me coming and talking with them, but the youngest of the group seemed to like me, his name was Kyle. Kyle and I went on to have many conversations about "Jesus not starting a religion". He confided in me that he was raised in church in the south, and that he wanted nothing to do with religion but he was open to hearing about Jesus.

I said, "Jesus loves you Kyle. It's just that simple. He isn't interested in controlling you. He wants to set you free. It's exactly the opposite of what you learned in those religious places throughout the south. Jesus is the only way to God. There is no other. Not even religion can get us to God." Kyle was all ears. It was obvious that he didn't really want that life. He had just never found what he was looking for, he never found the real Jesus. I told Him about the Goodness of God and His Mercy. I told Kyle as much as I knew about *The Real Jesus* and Kyle started to hope again!

One day Kyle said, "What must I do to be saved?" I told him, "It's not hard. Just tell the Lord you don't want this life anymore, receive Jesus into your heart and be baptized; and you will be saved!" It was Easter 2014 when Kyle came over to my apartment and asked to be baptized. I called John and the three of us went to a beautiful spot on the beach, where the sea turtles like to gather in the rocks. We baptized Kyle unto Christ. I will never forget Kyle and the day he was baptized. It's forever engrained into my heart.

The sky was exceptionally dramatic that day, the sun bursting through the clouds, the water wasn't as still as it normally was and Kyle was like a child, jumping around, so happy to be giving his life to Jesus. It was clear to me that Kyle had never wanted to become a drug dealer. It had just sort of happened. His dad had gotten him started in meth when he was eleven or so and the two of them started selling it to afford their habit and lifestyle. Standing there on the beach watching Kyle rush into the water to meet Jesus, I silently said to The Lord, "This is what I want to do for the rest of my life . . ." I was so happy for Kyle!

I said a simple prayer and let Kyle say the rest. His prayer couldn't have been any better. He said, "I am sorry for all that I have done Lord. I don't want to be like this anymore. Please change me forever. Please receive me into your family. I want to be with you from now on." And he didn't wait for me to dunk him in the ocean, he jumped right in it! It was really a miracle. Kyle was immediately healed of his drug addiction. And he even stopped smoking.

Soon thereafter, Kyle's dad got off meth and started to walk with God too. Day by day God changed their family. It turned out that they were nothing like the stereo-typical drug dealers on television. They were broken-hearted and hurting, lost and alone, but they were not horrible people. Like the rest of us, Kyle and his dad just needed to be loved. I praise Jesus that He gave me the grace to conquer my fears and to go over and love them.

I came to learn that Kyle was actually a very innocent young man with a good heart, and he immediately became a minister. It was wild to watch. One day we were driving down the road and Kyle yelled out, "Stop! I have to minister to that girl!" I said, "Who? Where?" He pointed to some girl seated next to a gas station. I pulled into the gas station even though I had no real urge by the Holy Spirit. But I trusted Kyle.

Kyle said, "What do I say to her!?" I said, "Just pray that the Lord gives you something to say that will minister to her." He prayed and shot out of the car like a rocket headed to its target! Kyle was overjoyed when he came back to the car a few moments later. God gave Kyle only the words, "Jesus loves you. Did you know that?" When he asked her she replied, "No. I never heard that before." And she took off her glasses. That morning she had been beaten up pretty badly by her boyfriend. She really needed to hear that God loved her that morning. Kyle was God's instrument in ministering to that young girl. He had only been saved a couple of days. Kyle prayed for her, as if he had been praying for people by the side of the road for years, and returned to tell me the good news.

Kyle left shortly after his life had changed to return to Oklahoma and be reunited with his son and his son's mother. Even though his trip did not go at all according to his plan and he was very hurt by all that happened with his son's mother, he did not return to drugs; but continued on with Jesus. Kyle runs a motel now in Oklahoma and is still growing in his faith, day by day. His dad is still walking with Jesus and living in Hawaii. I will love these guys forever. They are precious children of God!

Δ Ω

David, John and I had many more adventures together with the power of God. One of David's friends was set free of homosexuality while we were all together. I had a week of what we called, "Glory Meetings" where God would show up every night for a week! It was awesome. We were seeing God's love regularly poured out during our time together. But after Kyle left there was a noticeable change.

The church that David was a part of was coming against him without a cause. And God started to minister to us all that David's time in Hawaii was coming to an end. About the same time David was getting ready to leave, the Lord started to tell us that He was moving us on also. After David flew back to California, we moved to the north side of the island and were grafted into a whole new group of people.

I was given grace to minister often while we were up north. The Lord showed me His love towards this new generation as I started to minister along side of a youth pastor, a new friend of mine named Chris. But the religion up there was so old and engrained that it was very difficult to get any movement in the Spirit. Every time the Lord would really start to break out that *religious spirit* would show up to try to stifle Him. It was hard not to be irritated seeing what was happening. I had to really fight the urge of wanting to return to *the rage-machine*. It seemed like we were so close again to Revival breaking out but something kept coming against us. Ugh! Not fun!

I urged Chris to come away from his desire to please the men of that religion. But he kept encouraging me to become a pastor of their denomination. It was a disagreement that would eventually drive us apart. I served with all my heart while on the north side of the island, but in the end God moved us on.

One day we were at the beach resting, when two women and a man with a dog approached us. I felt the Lord in it so I started some small talk. Every time I thought I found an opening to minister the conversation would shift. So I remained patient.

As they were getting ready to leave the Lord practically yelled at me, "Tell her not to give up on her husband yet. I am dealing with him." I said to the woman who the Lord had spoken about, "The Lord just told me to tell you not to give up on your husband just yet. He wants you to know that He is still working on him." The woman looked at me with such surprise and started to weep. She never mentioned anything about her husband or her life back at home but in fact she had come to Hawaii to decide whether or not to divorce him. There was no word from God I could have given her that would have ministered to her any better. It was another genuine Jesus miracle.

Months later I ran into her friend in the grocery store. Her friend told me that she decided to start believing in Jesus again after she saw what God did that day. She said, "Thank you. I will never leave Him again. Now I know for sure that Jesus is truly the Son of God!" We couldn't help but weep together in the grocery store; amazed at God's love for us. From what I last heard that woman is still with her husband to this day.

The ministry to the youth was incredible. God dumped His love on them every time we would meet. Even with all the religiosity around us, The Spirit of God was stronger. Many of those kids received a faith in Jesus that would never be stolen away from them. But like I said, in the end that old religious spirit was coming against us and God pulled us out of that place. Shirley and I knew our days in Hawaii were quickly coming to an end. We knew that we were being sent out again but we didn't know to where. We started praying diligently.

We had to fast and pray and wait. It took a full month until finally we had it confirmed to us that we would be headed to the beautiful Pacific Northwest. It was like a warzone around the island as we prepared to leave. We were kicked out a brother in the Lord's place where we were staying when Shirley and the girls all had the stomach flu. It was a horrible day! But the Lord helped us. Another brother, a Russian brother, Kerry and his wife Kat saved us. We love the Russians!

The intensity of the spiritual battle was almost more than I could handle as we were making our way off the island. I just kept praying and sometimes fasting. I wanted to leave immediately but God continued to slow us down. To this day I don't know why He was slowing us down?

Then suddenly it was all over and we were on a flight headed to Portland, Oregon. I was beyond happy to be leaving the beautiful islands of Hawaii . . .

I knew that we were on the way to our Promised Land!

Chapter 20

If I said that this incredible journey with the Lord was easy I wouldn't be telling the truth. These years have been many things, but easy would not be one of the words to describe them. Words I would use to describe my time with the Lord would be: awe-inspiring, sorrowful, joyous, heartbreaking, unimaginable, dreamy, majestic and glorious. I set out with the hope of changing things that I did not like in the world, especially within the church, but it was me who ended up changing. I can't say how much Jesus changed this world through me? But I can say He made me a completely new person. And I am so grateful for it!

I would encourage anyone with enough courage to wrestle it out with the Lord. I would encourage anyone who has enough guts to go and work out their salvation with fear and trembling. Jacob wrestled with the angel of the Lord and a nation was born soon after. The word *Israel* literally interpreted means, "To wrestle or struggle with the Lord." Now in Christ, grafted into the original olive tree, we are also those who "wrestle" it out with God. We have an incredible gift in Christ! We are the ones chosen to be the children of *The Most High God* . . . The ones who get to know Him, intimately.

So it's not supposed to be easy, wrestling with God. It's not necessarily supposed to be enjoyable all the time either, but the rewards are more than worth it, and the view from the top is truly breath-taking. Even still, there is so much more. We serve an everlasting and infinite God. So I would encourage all of you brothers to go as the Lord leads. Trust Him and He will bring you to life and life everlasting. He never promised it would be an easy journey but He did say that He will always be with us, every step of the way; even if we fall ... He will be with us!

I have some more of the story to tell before I finish writing.

Δ   Ω

We arrived in Portland without any real direction but for once we had a good friend of mine picking us up from the airport, Gary, my dearest friend from Arizona. Gary had moved to Portland and was happy to be reuniting with me for another round of adventures with Jesus.

The Lord kept confirming to me that He had a word for me to deliver to the Russian Church in Portland. I told Gary the whole story, and along with Shirley we started to pray that the Lord would open a door for us. (It's much better to wait on the Lord; wait for Him to open a door rather than for us to try to open it ourselves.) One Saturday morning Gary felt especially inspired. He had stayed up late into the night searching for Russian Churches, and he had made a list for us to go and visit.

Being that it was a Saturday, I knew that it would take a miracle for us to find someone around; obviously Christian churches on the whole, meet on Sundays. I prayed over Gary's list and felt a special draw to one name. We headed for that church first. As we arrived there we saw that the name had changed. It didn't seem to be a Russian church at all, but the parking lot was full so I decided to go inside and see what was happening.

There was a Russian Church meeting inside. I couldn't believe it! They were in the middle of a service of some kind and I decided to join in. Shirley waited in the car with the girls while they slept. Gary came inside with me. I motioned to someone who seemed to be pastoral and he met me in the back of the church to talk for a brief moment. I explained to him that the Lord had given me this word for the Russian Church and that I needed a moment to share it. He agreed to let me speak.

As the service ended he grabbed the microphone and introduced me to the congregation before the senior pastor and gave me the microphone. I started to explain to them that the Lord wants unity. He wants unity in all the churches, black churches, white churches, Russian Churches and American Churches. I went on to preach a short exhortation, and then the Spirit of the Lord came upon me. I started to apologize on the behalf of the American Church for sometimes not treating the Russian Church like brothers... as I did, I wept. I prayed for unity between our churches, and as I did, the pastors must have felt the power of God too.

The senior pastor took up a microphone and also started to apologize and weep together with me, thanking the American Church for often being very good to him and his fellow Russians. He apologized for keeping himself separated from us at times. He wept as he spoke about God's desire for unity in His Church. It was a very moving time. The Spirit of God was very thick in the room and many of the congregation wept along with us, Gary too. There was something very holy going on it the church that day.

As we finished what the Lord put on our hearts, a very old woman, probably in her 80's, stood up, somewhat shaky because she was so moved by the Spirit. She said something in Russian. As she spoke many of the congregation started to Praise God and shout, "Hallelujah!" I was overwhelmed again and again with the presence of God. One of the pastors finally started to translate to me what had happened. He said, "The old lady reminded the pastor that she had called him early in the morning to tell him that the Lord had given her a vision around 4:00 a.m. In the vision she saw you, she said. You were dressed like a soldier and very strong in appearance. Then the Lord told her. "I am sending this man to you. Listen to what he says. He has a message for the whole Russian Church." As it turned out, the pastor had forgotten the whole thing until she stood up shaking, reminding him about what a great thing the Lord had just done.

Every time God shows up it is incredible. No matter how many times the Lord shows up and does amazing things it is awe inspiring. No matter how often I see Him moving, He still takes my breath away. His love, His mercy and His goodness are just so wonderful, I can't help but be amazed. It is such a pleasure to be with Him.

But that would not be the only spectacular thing the Lord would have me to proclaim in Portland...

Δ   Ω

We left Gary's house shortly after the Lord moved with the Russians, and we were put up in a hotel for a week. During that time, I woke up early on Sunday morning, and while in prayer, the Lord said, "I have somewhere for you to preach today." I laughed joyfully and said, "Just tell me where to go!" Shirley and the girls were still sleeping but I whispered in my wife's ear, "I'm going to preach. I will be back later." Shirley by then was more than accustomed to my unique ways of following Jesus. She just smiled, obviously thinking 'you have nowhere to preach today'? But she knew better than to try to stop me, so she said, "Have fun honey. I'll see you when you get back." (And to answer your question, No, it was not always that easy to have Shirley trust me and follow me as I follow after the Lord. But she has done a tremendous job. She is truly one-of-a-kind!)

I walked out of the hotel around 7:30 a.m. and went to find where I would be preaching. I walked to a major intersection and was about to go left when the Lord said clearly, "No. Go right." I turned right and started praying, proclaiming something that the Lord had put on my heart, I said, "I speak to the four winds of heaven and I say blow upon the church! Blow upon the dry bones and cause them to come to life. Awaken your mighty army, O Lord! Awaken the sleeping Army of God and raise up your sons!" It was a very powerful time walking down the side of the road proclaiming the words of God, proclaiming to the dead bones to come to life.

As I came near to a certain hotel the Lord said, "Go inside. There is a church that meets there every Sunday. They will let you preach the word I have given you." I went inside and spoke with the girl at the front desk, I said, "I was walking down the street praying and I heard the Lord say to come in here and preach. Is there a church who meets here?" She looked astonished. She said, "Yes! But they don't advertise. So it would have had to be the Lord directing you here!" She was a believer and started to glorify the name of God. As she did, the Holy Spirit fell upon us both. She decided that she would make sure the pastor was expecting me when I returned. They did not start for another hour and a half so I went home to get Shirley and the girls.

We returned to the church and they received us gladly. When my time came to speak, I opened the word of God to Ezekiel 37 and started to prophesy. Then I turned to Joel, Chapter 2 and I started to prophesy again. As I prophesied the whole church came to life and shouted and gave God the glory. I didn't really know the whole story of what was making them so excited until I finished prophesying and sat down.

The pastor came to the pulpit and wanted to explain to me why everyone was so overjoyed with my message. He said, "You see last week I preached from Joel Chapter 2 and the week before that I preached from Ezekiel 37." He continued, "God is really telling us something very important here. He is telling us that *now* is the time indeed that He is going to manifest His sons! He just confirmed it with the words of two of His servants." I agreed together with the whole congregation, and we praised the holy name of God, again and again, and prayed over all that had just happened. It was a time of incredible joy and celebration.

The Lord gave us a little more grace to minister at a few other churches in Portland but we left not long after that. I had awoken one Monday morning a few weeks after we ministered at the hotel church. The Lord said, "You are leaving Portland today." I asked, "To where Lord?" After interpreting a recent dream of Shirley's we realized that we were headed to Seattle!

It was the beginning of 2015. It was Jubilee. The time appointed when God would make all things new: the time appointed when God would restore everything!

Δ   Ω

What would become of us, Church, if we were to keep ourselves hidden within the walls of the institutions? What would become of the precious gospel of Jesus Christ if we were to remain, merely, religious? So God is separating unto Himself a remnant. He is calling us out. He is making, for His Kingdom, sons, heirs of righteousness and joint-heirs of Christ. He is God... and He is about to make Himself known again, He is about to reveal His Goodness for the whole world to see!

Jesus never started a religion; He restored us to our Father; He restored the family of God. Now He is bringing us unto the fullness. He is completing the work He began in us so long ago, (*Romans 11:25*)! He has always had this plan in mind. He was always going to extend grace towards our religion, but then in the time appointed, He would judge it.

"Do you see the buildings of the temple?" He told them, "Not one stone shall be left upon another for all shall be thrown down." (Matthew 24) That temple always represented false religion and Jesus was explaining to His disciples, among other things, that before His return, He was going to judge the false religion. He told them that He was going to tear it down! God never asked for that temple to be built. Study it for yourselves. (II Samuel 7) David wanted it and then Solomon built it and while God went along with them, He never asked for it and He never wanted it to be built. God wanted a tabernacle "But Solomon built Him a house." (Acts 7:47) Return to these scriptures for yourselves.

The first church knew this message. They knew very well that God never wanted the temple, because Jesus taught them these things and the Holy Spirit helped to reveal it to them. Why was Stephen martyred? Read the story again. (Acts 6 and 7) He had judged their temple. Standing right outside the temple he preached boldly and proclaimed the word of the Lord, "God wanted a tabernacle, but Solomon built Him a house. Howbeit the Most High does not dwell in temples made by hands, as says the prophet, Heaven is my throne and the earth my footstool, what house will you build unto me? And where is the place of my rest?" (Isaiah 66:1, 2; Acts 7:47–50) Then the religious leaders heard him and grew so angry they grabbed him and dragged him outside the temple and stoned him to death. The first martyr of the church was martyred for judging this false religion.

God does not bless our religious additions or deletions to His Word. He is a God of order, lights and perfection. He never wanted anything to come in between His relationship with us. That includes all of the religious stuff. He is Jealous for us. He wants that nothing would get in His way of Him Fathering us. So the last idolatry that must go is, *The Religion. And Oh, How hard it will be for men to let go of it*!

There will be no temple in heaven. There will be no denominations and no more divisions; in heaven we will finally be the family of God. But wait! THE KINGDOM OF HEAVEN IS AT HAND! God wants us to live His kingdom today. Dear brothers, let us live firmly planted in eternity not after this life has ended but today! None of this fallen world is coming with us. Somewhere in our hearts we know this. We are safe with Him. Everything is going to be Ok. My testimony is only an example of how safe we are, trusting our Father. I wrote this testimony to inspire a generation to fully hope in their God! Watch! He is manifesting His sons!

And we must wait for Him. We cannot do these things on our own. He will move the mountains; we will speak to them but He will move them. The battle is the Lord's. We must become mature and wait upon His leading. He is still the Shepherd and we are still His sheep. Then as the Shepherd speaks, *The sheep will hear His voice*. Rest in His Word brothers, and He will put you out into His vineyard, out into the fields to harvest. He will bring the good works out of us to glorify His holy name!

Now every good soldier knows to obey the voice of his Captain.

"Wait, I say, Wait upon the Lord."

△ Ω

It's very natural and fleshly to build as our fathers have built, and as their fathers built, and their fathers before them. But then God shows up in the midst of all this striving and toil; and He shows us the futility of all our efforts. None of what we build in this earth will be found in heaven. So what on this earth then matters? There is a time to build and also a time to tear down (Ecclesiastes 3:5). But where will we be building? Let us return to the beginning and be reminded.

Adam sinned and then he hid himself. What was he afraid of? What had God ever done to him that would cause His son to feel afraid? The answer is of course, nothing. Adam was afraid because he had already received the curse, having disobeyed the voice of God, he had already received the wages of sin. Perhaps Adam had never known what it was to fear before the fall. So when Adam's loving Father came, Adam, having been overcome by the flesh, *hid himself.* (Genesis 3)

And the curse spread and covered the earth. Man continued to run and hide away from their God and Father. Cain killed Abel. And the curse spread, until there was only one man left on earth found righteous in the eyes of God. Every other man on earth was content to do wickedness before the Lord without fear, without repentance. The flesh had all but completely destroyed God's creation. (Genesis 6)

Then even after the flood the curse started to work its wickedness in the hearts of men once more. Men were so afraid they said, "Come, let us make for ourselves a city, a name and a tower whose top may reach unto heaven, lest we be scattered abroad the face of the whole earth." Men did not build Babel because they trusted in the goodness of God and His true love for them, men built Babel because they were afraid, because they did not believe that God is good. They built that name and city and tower in hopes to preserve their own lives because they did not trust in God. (Genesis 11)

And men have not stopped building Babel ever since. For fear, men labor and toil greatly upon the face of the earth. Men continue to build this Babel hoping to preserve their lives. Especially many of the rich, they are some of the most fearful among us. And the curse has all but covered the earth once more. Babel, which in the Greek tongue is Babylon, must be removed off of the face of the earth. Our Father will remove it in His time.

What else have men built upon the earth for fear? What other ungodly horrors have men established upon God's majestic creation for fear of being scattered? What if instead of this fear, His love was the anchor of our souls? What would we build if we trusted in His love and we were no longer afraid? What would we labor after if we knew the goodness of our God?

Men of God, Paul warned us, "Take heed how you build upon this foundation." Paul said, "Be careful what kind of a life you build, brothers." We will build one kind of a structure being overcome by our fears but we will build such glory and beauty being overcome by the love of God. We must come away from this curse; this flesh must be made into something new. In Christ we have been given this victory. But outside of Christ there is only the curse. (I Corinthians 3)

Men build religion because they are afraid; because they are convinced that God needs their works. Men build religion, not understanding just how powerful and capable our Father truly is. Men build religion just as those men built Babel after the flood, they were afraid: "What will become of us?" they say among themselves. And so they labor and toil all the days of their lives, never coming to know the fullness of the love of God. Eating of the tree of the knowledge of good and evil, they forsake the tree of life. These men will truly live under a curse until the end. This is not the love of God in Christ Jesus that we have been given.

We have such victory in Christ. Jesus came that we might be returned to our Father as we were with Him in the garden. Jesus came to restore our place of intimacy and fellowship with Him, that we would know His love for us is true. There was no temple in the garden because God was in perfect fellowship with men. There will be no temple in heaven because men will once again be in perfect fellowship with their Father. And the kingdom of heaven is at hand!

Jesus has already fought and won for us this victory. We have already been restored to our Father. We are only just waking to this Truth. We are only just starting to receive our inheritance. This is the beginning of something new. God is our Father in Jesus mighty name! We do not need any man to help us to approach Him; in the same way my children need no help in coming to me. Jesus is the Way to the Father. Our Father loves us. We are His. We have been totally restored unto Him, both now and forever! Amen.

Men build religion because they do not understand the love of God; neither the power of His love. "There is no fear in love but perfect love casts out fear. For where there is fear there is also torment. He who fears is not yet made perfect in love." (I John 4:17) Men build religion because they have not yet been made perfect in the love of God and so they think that it's necessary. Men still believe religion is necessary for the survival of Jesus' Church. Many trust in the works of their own hands more than they trust in the Spirit of the Living God.

But God's love is being revealed anew. The love of God is being put on display in ways never before seen or heard of. "Greater works than these you shall do!" The Body of Christ is coming together in a unity that has not been seen for many generations, because God's love is being perfected in us! As His love is being poured out, the fear is leaving and what is left but true fellowship with the Spirit; and then finally the true fellowship of the saints.

Grab hold of your seats, Dear brothers and sisters.
It's going to get even better than this.
He is taking us to the fullness of His love.
It's a very exciting time to be alive, indeed!

Chapter 21

I remember the day that the Lord asked me, "Robert, do you think that I need anyone to teach you the gospel?" It was an odd question to me. But the obvious answer, since He *is* God, was, "No. You are God. You don't need anyone to teach me . . ." But I didn't understand what He was telling me at the time. All my life I had thought that we go to church services to find God. Quickly I started to learn just how incorrect a doctrine that is. God needs no man to teach us anything, as John wrote to us, "But the anointing that you have received abides in you, and just as it abides in you, you shall abide in Him. And you do not need that any man should teach you, but the anointing you have received of Him shall teach you all things." (I John 2:28). It was perhaps six months after the Lord asked me that question that I found this scripture. My Father was setting me free to walk with Him without encumbrance.

Of course the Lord has given to the Church: apostles, prophets, evangelists, pastors and teachers, to serve in the equipping of the saints. I am not writing a new gospel here, but an old one, the gospel given to us from the beginning: God is our Father and He loves us. He is constantly working to draw us closer to Himself and He is very Jealous for us; that is His name, *Jealous*. He would have that no one would come in between Him and His children, even those religious rulers. He is going to Father us and He sent us a Great Shepherd to keep us in His way.

We, of His Church, were always supposed to be serving one another in love. Bolstering and edifying one another further into the presence of God and the fullness of His love. But never were we to be ruling each other. Jesus did not establish a hierarchy, quite the contrary; He established a kingdom of servants and lovers. He even warned His apostles, "The kings of the gentiles exercise lordship over you and those who do are called [rulers], but with you, let it not be so, rather, whosoever would be the greatest among you let him be as the younger . . ." (Luke 22:25–30) These same words of our Lord are recorded in three of the four gospels. We were to be lover-servants of God, not rulers, not lords over His heritage.

But it feels so good to this flesh to lord over another man. This flesh loves the pride and feeling of power that comes with ruling and this kind of worldly authority. Our flesh despises humility, laying down our lives for our brother, suffering and any sort of sacrifice. This kind of life of surrender is completely not of this world. It never has been and it never will be. God is doing away with the flesh and making all things new. He is teaching us to lay down our lives for our brothers. He is teaching us to love, like He loves.

But some men will hold to the affairs of the religious world until the very end. They will, acting as their own gods, subject men unto themselves and their own will; even going so far as to call themselves 'Christ', which means Messiah. This wicked spirit is already among us. But God knows those who are His. Jesus knows everyone who has been promised unto Himself. He will save us. Have no fear. We are very safe with our All-Powerful, Loving Father.

We are so safe in fact that we can surrender our lives for the sake of His kingdom. We can lay our lives down upon His altar and He will make us into something very amazing, something beautiful. We are blessed and safe in Him. He has never failed us and He will never fail us. The One whom we follow after, the One seated upon the white horse, He is called, "Faithful and True!" He can be trusted. He is Good. He is revealing His Goodness now across the whole world, that every man might see Him and glorify His Christ.

We cannot take ourselves unto perfection! Our Father, through the power of His Holy Spirit, is going to bring us unto the fullness. We need only to receive of Him. To trust Him is to rest in Him. We alone, cannot finish the work He began in us. But we can obey. We can trust and we can obey.

Let us therefore come into this perfection in Christ, Holy Church.

Δ Ω

God's ways are higher than our ways, brothers. It is time we stop questioning His Word and instead start to trust Him and obey. These things are all received by faith. We do not first understand and then we obey, rather we first trust and obey by faith in the love of God, and then we start to understand.

"Abraham believed God and it was accounted unto him as righteousness." (James 2:23, Romans 4:3) Abraham did not wait until he had it all figured out to follow God. He believed and obeyed his word from God and for Abraham's faith he was highly rewarded. "But without faith it is impossible to please God." (Hebrews 11:6) In the same way God can keep His truths hidden from some, He can also reveal it unto babes. (Luke 10:21)

The greatest of the kingdom of God have always been the children. (Matthew 18) The children of God trust their Father, they believe in His goodness and so they remain by His side. But those wicked, prideful men continually doubt His love and question God's every intention; until finally they decide to stop following Him altogether. Let us not be as that wicked generation who perished in the wilderness having never believed in the word of their God. (Hebrews 3 & 4) But let us be the children of our Father, who believing in His Word receive our every promise fulfilled in Christ. Amen.

It's strange that we would need to convince ourselves that God knows better than we do, but our flesh is at such enmity against God that in truth, as men, we need to be reminded continually . . . God knows best. Our Father, who has neither beginning nor ending, who is both omnipotent and omnipresent, He knows all things. We might as well sit at His feet and learn from Him, obey His word and receive the blessing. This pride has never helped us to receive of Him.

Children do a better job than we do as mere *religious* men. Often they are quicker to repent when they realize that they have done something wrong, or if there is a better way to do something they change more easily. They are much more trusting. They are more willing to listen and take instruction. Children, especially when they know that they are loved, will follow their Father anywhere He might lead them. In Christ, we are so very fortunate being called, *the children of God.*

Jesus told us, "The Greatest among you is as this child."

It is therefore written, "A little child shall lead them."

$$\Delta \quad \Omega$$

Shirley, Goodness, Mercy and I have been in Seattle now for about a year. This has been one of the most rewarding years of my whole life. The Lord has shown me over and again, *Now it is time.* So after all these years of writing and learning, and rewriting, I am going to share what the Lord has been giving me: *Jesus didn't start a religion.*

Many of this generation are refusing to participate with the religious institutions. Many of those who are bearing with the old wine skins are not able to receive from them. And why? Because they are new wine skins. I have long seen the difference within the body of Christ. New wine skins are made to receive new wine, it's just that simple. But they say, "The old is better." And so they hold to what they know and reject what their God is doing, today but "Today is the day of salvation." Therefore, let us, "Sing unto the Lord a new song, and his praise from the ends of the earth . . ." (Isaiah 42:10)

Sometimes people ask me after hearing this bold message, "So what then did Jesus do?" I say, "He changed everything. He didn't merely start some religion; He gave us complete access again, to be the children of God!" Do you realize what that means? God is our Father again! The King of All Creation, The Creator of heaven and earth, God, He is our Father. And what

Good Father ignores His children? We have such an inheritance in our Christ with our God. Children are born into a family with a certain heritage. In Christ, what heritage are we born into? It's amazing to consider!

Jesus absolutely started something. He started many things in fact. He started His kingdom on the earth, within us. He took these twelve men and gave to them the kingdom of God. Then He began to manifest His kingdom upon the earth out of that first brotherhood. Jesus in fact changed everything. That is why the whole world knows His name and still talks about Him to this very day. His Kingdom is taking up residence even as you are reading the words off of this page.

But religion is altogether earthly. Religion does not establish His kingdom primarily, but secondarily or somewhere further down the list. Religion seeks to establish their own names, their own ways and their own doctrines upon the earth; sometimes in agreement with the word of God, but other times in disagreement. This religion seeks to control rather than let the Spirit of God be the guide. Brothers, this by no means, pleases our Father who gave up His Son to be a ransom for our souls.

Do we want our names written in heaven or on the earth? (Jeremiah 17:13) Who cares if we are known among men? What matters is that we are known unto God. Remember Jesus warning us about the people coming to Him and trying to justify themselves, giving to Him their list of accomplishments of what they did for His Kingdom but He will respond, "Depart from me, I never knew you." (Matthew 7:21-23)

Remember who killed our Lord and Savior? Was it not the religious rulers of the day? Rome tried as hard as they could to get out of crucifying our Christ, but the religious rulers stirred up the people and practically forced the hand of Rome to crucify their/our Savior. Brothers and sisters, many of these religious leaders would crucify Him again if they had the opportunity. Why? Because they love their positions and their earthly kingdoms more than they love the Lord who laid down His life for them. It's a very sad truth but a truth nonetheless.

Don't worry, His sheep will hear His voice and they will be known by their Shepherd.

Δ   Ω

I would love to tell you that this journey has not been hard on my heart. I would love to tell you that I have never been afraid walking by faith with Jesus out in the midst of the world, but that is not what I experienced. Even still, Paul suffered greatly and he counted it all as a privilege to be considered worthy to suffer for Christ. I have suffered little compared with these apostles. And my Christ suffered so much more. Any suffering I have endured by His grace has been my privilege and my blessing; and one day my reward! This is my trust in God.

If we seek to please men, we will have a very hard time pleasing God, but if we seek to please God, some men will be pleased and we will be a part of God's plan for salvation. Do not take one part of scripture and throw out another. God will give us grace to receive both the good and the suffering of this fallen world. He is "a very present Help in our time of trouble" (Psalm 46:1). The whole world suffers but in Christ we get to suffer as we participate in God's plan for salvation.

"For the joy set before Him Christ endured the cross!" (Hebrews 12:2) He saw His reward, what lay on the other side of the cross, and He was able to endure. We cannot imagine what rewards lay in store for us in eternity, but God will help us to see, even if only in part, what He is preparing for us in life everlasting. Jesus said, "Blessed are those who believe without seeing." It is truly our honor to be counted worthy to suffer alongside our Lord. In heaven we will see more clearly.

But it isn't all bad news. There is so much good news. Reread all the testimonies of the saints. Reread what God has done over the generations, with lives laid down in surrender to His Spirit. God takes us as broken vessels and works His glory out of our lives to bring salvation in Jesus name to this broken world. We get to be the heirs of salvation. That is why we are called, "The Body of Christ". When people see His Church living out His love, it is like they are seeing a part of Jesus Himself. *But who is willing to give of their lives?*

In heaven, standing before Him when it is all finished, we are going to wish we had believed fully. Standing there in His presence, seeing His power, His majesty and His love we are going to weep because we are going to see, "It's all true. The whole story. The love of God. Jesus Christ *is* seated at the right hand of the power. He really is a Good God." And we are going to weep because we only believed in Him a little bit. We will mourn for a moment because we will wish we had given to Him everything.

But Jesus will come near to us and He will wipe the tears from our eyes and He will comfort us, who are His children. In His presence there will be no shame, no condemnation, no regret, but only love and acceptance; all the former things will be forgotten and they will be remembered no more. He will receive us and say, "Well done my good and faithful servant. Come and inherit the kingdom that I have prepared for you from before the foundations of the earth." And then we will be with Him, together, forever.

Now it is the time to labor. Now is the time of salvation. There will come a day when the door will be shut and there will be no more salvation, but judgment; but that is not today. Today is the day of salvation. Let us go and be faithful with these precious things which we have been given. Freely we have received, now freely let us go and give.

Let us not be as the false religious ones, like those Pharisees hell bent on judgment, but let us be as our Lord and Savior, quick to forgive and pass out God's mercy. We are here to intercede for the lost ones of the world. We are here to make intercession before the throne of God for this lost and dying world. There will come a time for judgment but that is not today. Today is the time of Mercy, the time to forgive sins, the time to give to every man, woman and child who would receive . . . Redemption in Jesus holy name!

The judgment will come and the books will be opened and every man will be judged out of those things written in the books (Revelation 20). But it won't be us! The Redeemed will not stand in judgment for we have become the heirs of salvation upon whom the judgment will *Passover*. We are set apart, both now and forever. Amen.

Now let us add to the number in Christ that every man who hears this gospel might be saved from the judgment and hell-fire to come. Let us preach the true gospel in faith, knowing that this religion has never had the power to save, but only Christ. There remains no other name by which men can be saved. So let us call upon His holy name and be made The Redeemed of the Lord!

And those who know His name they call Him, Jesus!

Δ   Ω

Shirley, Goodness, and Mercy are asleep in the other room as I am writing to you, praying about the final things that the Lord would have me to say. It's late in the evening here but soon the son will rise; the morning star will come in glory for the children of God!

Children are trusting and vulnerable, children are open hearted and innocent, children are pure and like virgins, undefiled. Let us not seek to be knowledgeable but full of life. In the garden they turned away from the tree of life to go after knowledge, *the knowledge of both good and evil*. Let us rather be innocent, white as doves, pure as the driven snow. Let us be "wise as serpents and gentle as doves".

It's going to take a lot of heart to make it out of this world alive. So God will break our hearts that He might fill us again to overflowing. He will break us open to enlarge our hearts, that we might love them more. He will break through our hearts of stone to give us hearts of flesh and blood. We have not, because we ask not. Let us ask for His love and He will give it to us.

The only power that will win this lost and dying world is His love. Faith alone will not do it. For it is written, "By this shall

all men know that you are my disciples, if you have love one to another." (John 13:35) They will not necessarily know us by our faith that removes mountains and awakens the dead. But they will know us by our love, because *God is love.* This is the same gospel you have heard from the beginning. The greatest among us will be servant-lovers of the body of Christ! And "many of the least among you will be the greatest in the kingdom of God." It's blessed to be the children of God; and it's much easier than trying to be God.

Everything written to us in the scriptures is true. But we are in a time wherein men will not listen to sound doctrine. Be warned. Men would rather exalt for themselves teachers who will teach according to their own wicked hearts desires, but "wisdom is justified in her children." The scripture says, not in vain, "Come out from among them and be ye separate." God will lead you to the brothers and sisters with whom you should be assembled.

Gather yourselves together and all the more as you see the day approaching. (Hebrews 10:25) Do not separate yourselves sensually as is the occasion of some but come together in holiness and in truth, waiting upon the Holy Spirit and He will come to you. God has given the Church gifts for the edifying of the saints and the encouragement to the Body of Christ. Until the day that we are brought into perfection, come together encourage one another in Christ and love one another.

To love is to give. The man who says that he loves his brother but then withholds his goods from him has deceived himself. (I John 3:17) Love is like a good servant who is always seeking to meet the needs of those given unto him. A good servant knows how to sacrifice of himself. And "greater love has no man than he would lay down his life for his friends."

I heard an elder in the faith once say, "Die Empty." Let us finish the race having poured out everything we have upon the altar, our lives having become a pleasing offering unto our God. Such is a life well lived. In eternity we will be grateful that He gave us such grace.

May you be provoked Church, unto Good Works that will glorify the name of Jesus. Christ will be our reward as we seek to abide in the goodness of our God.

It is a good gospel. It's simple. Jesus loves us!

Let's us go and preach it!

Chapter 22

I tell you these stories, and maybe it sounds like I was born with this unbelievable faith or some special gift. Certainly God gave me gifts but I believe the best gifts God gives us are not what we usually hope for. I was given this insatiable hunger, wanting to know Him more; I have an endless thirst, wanting more of His everlasting life inside of me. I have been given a childlike nature and a childlike persistence. But I think the greatest gift God gave me is that I always want to be with Him. These are the first and the best gifts that God put inside of me; the gifts of faith or the other gifts of the Spirit I received seemed to come along much later.

As a child I really believed in the goodness of God. I saw Him doing amazing things all around me and I really wanted to know Him. Over the years, I read many different books and studied many different schools of thought, but it all leads me back to the simplicity of Christ. I have known betrayal and heart-ache, but never by my Father. I have come to few conclusions but one I hold to is: there is no other man worth living for, there is no one else who can measure up to Jesus! There is no one who can come close to comparing, Jesus is just that Good. He is my God, He is my Father and there is no other!

Another conclusion I have come to: *He is God and I am not.* Perhaps that sounds funny? Perhaps you are thinking, who would think of himself as God? But there was a time that I was acting first and asking God later. The Lord never bailed out on me then but He taught me, like a Father teaches his son, the way of life, to surrender. Most of my twenties were lived without much Godly fear, doing whatever seemed *right in my own eyes*

(Judges 21:25). Then the Lord, in His mercy, showed me what I was doing and I repented. After all these years I have begun to really enjoy having my God, my Father, in my life. I have only recently begun to be truly obedient to His perfect will.

Obedience often sounds like a scary religious word, and I have heard it often taken out of context, or taught out of a wrong attitude. Obedience simply means, my Father knows better than me and He loves me, so I will listen to Him. Typically when our culture hears words like rules, laws or commandments, they take off running the other way. Everyone has rules that they accept in their lives. The argument has never been over rules but *whose rules we agree to follow*. Remember the first sin, man wanting to be his own God.

We all accept "the law of gravity" and so we rarely jump out of airplanes without a parachute. Most will receive laws of morality, like do unto others as you would have them to do unto you. For the most part we will obey laws of the land for fear of the law, for the fear of consequences, going to jail, etc. But what about God's commands? Why do we have such a problem following Him? He loves us. What's our problem? Maybe we have been poorly taught? Why don't we trust Him . . .

In Hebrew the word "Dabar" is often translated, "Commandment", but it is also translated "Word", like the "Word of the Lord". So let's substitute "Word" for the word "Law". Instead of saying "God's Law" let's say, "God's Word", because in our culture it's easier on the ears. So what if God's *Word* was in fact good for us? His word therefore would have never been to harm us but to help us, to give us the way to Life and Life Everlasting. How differently we would read the Word of God if we understood that He loves us and that He isn't trying to "pull a fast one" on us. Would we finally surrender to Him, obey His commands and trust Him with our lives?

What if it's all true and God is, in fact, just as loving as His Word declares that He is? If my dad loved me perfectly I would like to think that eventually he would earn my trust and I would start to listen to him. If he loved me perfectly, wouldn't I at some point in time start to listen and obey his voice? Perhaps our earthly fathers have done a bad job at showing us Christ and His goodness, but our Father has not done a bad job! He has never failed us. Not once. When we come to know His love for us is true, we will desire His Word and we will long for His Commands, just like King David. And we will be blessed, just like David the King!

Try to count how many times King David wrote about the goodness of God's Word. Read all the Psalms wherein the goodness of His Word/Law/Command is expressed, "Thy word have I hid in my heart that I might not sin against thee." Also, "I will delight myself in thy commandments, which I have loved." And, "O how I love thy law! It is my meditation all the day." (Psalm 119) I have had it so very wrong for much of my life, God is Good. His Word is Good. His Commands are Good. He loves me. He loves us. He isn't trying to harm us, He is bringing us unto life, and life everlasting! He is wanting to bless us!

I have often taught that coming to walk with God is like learning to play an instrument, let's say a piano. In the beginning we learn rudimentary things like, don't destroy the piano, don't light it on fire, don't smash it into pieces, etc. As we start to learn to play we learn simple scales and chords. Nothing complicated. But our Teacher is leading into playing Mozart and then to compose a beautiful symphony of our own. How differently would we listen to the voice of God if we knew that He is loving us into blessing and not cursing! How easily would we surrender to His Teaching if we knew that He is coaching us into becoming a masterpiece?

The Spirit of the Living God has been given to us. By the Spirit of God, thru Christ Jesus, we have been given the power to walk with God! This is also a part of the Good News! God is bringing us to blessing and away from cursing! All these things are received in Christ, by His Holy Spirit.

The children of God will hear me.

Δ Ω

The problems of religion are vast; the problems of false religion are even worse. If God is our Father then He is near to us; we can approach Him and come to live with Him. We don't need men to rule us. We don't need a leader or a middle-man between us and our God, Jesus is the way! We don't need generation's old establishments and institutions telling us what is, or is not the true doctrine. It's God's Word. We need the Spirit of the Living God. Our Father loves us, and thru Christ we get to have this amazing relationship with Him. He isn't far away. He is approachable. He is planted inside of us. He is our God and we are His people! We are His children.

The assemblies, the fellowship, the church gathered together, they are all supposed to point us into further intimacy and closeness with our God. The Bible was written to give us the way and reveal to us The Truth. The Word of God is Living, and He is constantly pointing us toward being exactly who He made us to be; in fullness, the children of God. Our Father gave us all this, including the gifts of apostles, prophets, evangelists, pastors and teachers; to serve us, to coach us into becoming His precious family, as servants. And just so we are clear, *He is The Father*. He has given us older men to serve the younger men, to teach them and to show them the way to life and life everlasting. But He is the Father!

I like to be called brother because He is The Father, He is the True Shepherd, He is my Pastor, He is our Teacher, He is our Accountability, He is our Hope, He is the True Prophet, He is the Apostle of our Salvation, He is my Lord and my Savior, before Him there is no other. It's His name that matters. But I would be more than happy to be your brother. I would be happy to walk with Jesus with you brothers!

God has a plan to save us. His Word, His Commandments, all lead us to this incredible and holy salvation! The last enemy to be defeated will be the death at work within this flesh; and the flesh will be put away forever (I Corinthians 15:35-56). We can trust Him. He is a Good God. He will not let us down. He will not fail us. He has never failed us. One day we will see more clearly.

He is bringing us home. It's going to be wonderful! We will see soon enough.

God is making for Himself sons. His sons will have one Father, one Savior, one Lord and one Shepherd of their souls. Return to the gospel that was originally given to us. Let us come to live in the fullness of this covenant promise we have received of Him!

Δ   Ω

Jesus took twelve men and taught them to be brothers. He taught them to agree. Among brothers, who is the ruler? Perhaps the eldest rules at times but it wasn't so with Joseph, or David the King, it wasn't so with Timothy; even Jesus was a young man when He began His ministry among the people and the elders, surely some of His disciples were older than He? Jesus didn't create a new religion, He created a brotherhood; He taught us to be the sons of God. And if I am a son and you are a son, then that makes us ... ?

Here is a good scripture for you, "If a man say, I love God, and hateth his brother, he is a liar: for he that loveth not his brother whom he hath seen, how can he love God whom he hath not seen?" (I John 4:20) But most of us have not been taught to be brother's, most of us have been prepared to be rulers, or to be ruled. This is at the foundation of that fallen religion, who is your ruler? "Father, let Your Holy Spirit have rule of me. Let your Word be my guide. Help me to surrender to Your ways and not the ways of this fallen world, the ways of the flesh. Help us Father. We need more of Jesus. Amen."

There remain divisions because men cannot agree. Men do not agree because they each live by their own word, by their own law, with their own god. Men do not "submit themselves one to another" in humility, we usually do not "in lowliness of mind each esteem others better than ourselves". We have a Father. We have a Good Father. As the Spirit of the Living God has His way within us, we will come to agree; just as they came to agree by the Spirit just after Pentecost. It's going to take a lot of fruit of the Spirit to live this way, brothers.

"And there was also strife among them, which of them should be accounted the greatest. And [Jesus] said unto them The kings of the Gentiles exercise lordship over them; and they that exercise authority upon them are called benefactors. But ye shall not be so: but he that is greatest among you, let him be as the younger; and he that is chief, as he that doth serve. For whether is greater, he that sitteth at meat, or he that serveth? Is not he that sitteth at meat? But I am among you as he that serveth. Ye are they which have continued with me in my temptations." (Luke 22:24–30) This is our kingdom brothers; this is the kingdom of our Father.

But it's faster and easier to build a kingdom on the earth. No doubt. It's easier to assemble men to follow, to build something with their hands, to remind men of their fear and wrestle them into submission. It's easier to live as the world lives in submission to our flesh, but the regret that comes along with that life, in the end, is unbearable. But to know that we poured out our lives upon His altar as a living sacrifice, having emptied ourselves unto death . . . that truly is a life worth living!

I feel like I am only just now learning to lay down my life for the brothers. I am only learning this love, "Greater love hath no man than this, that a man lay down his life for his friends." (John 15:13) It truly feels better, to the flesh, to rule rather than to serve, no doubt. But the rewards of the kingdom of God, the blessing, the abundance, the joy, the unity, the salvation, these things come through surrender; these things are found as a man *lays down his life for his friends*. But who is willing to do that?

God is making for Himself sons; sons who are like their Father. Jesus was/is the first born of many sons, He was/is the *only begotten* of the Father and Jesus is going to present others like Himself, as brothers, to His Dad. Some of you are leaping out of your seats reading this. The Spirit has so much more to give us as God Manifests His sons. Until then:

"The earnest expectation of the creature waiteth for the manifestation of the sons of God." (Romans 8:19)

Δ Ω

Jesus is returning for a bride made ready. He is coming back for a completed church, His family prepared for heaven. We might have come out of dysfunctional families, but through His Holy Spirit we are being made into something new, a glorious and loving family. We are becoming the family of God.

Good families live in agreement. Dads and moms shouldn't war against each other because they are *One Flesh*. (For those who have an ear to hear, this *One Flesh* is Christ and His Church.) The family of God will live in agreement! Then He sent them out, two by two. But "can two walk together, except they be agreed?" (Amos 3:3) Two brothers, walking in the unity of the Spirit were able to bring salvation to a countless many people! And "a three folded cord is not easily broken." (Ecclesiastes 4:12) "One will put a thousand to flight and two will send the legions fleeing." (Deuteronomy 32:30) Our Father is teaching us to be brothers! Isn't this an incredible story!?

So many of these gifts of the Spirit come by waiting... waiting and receiving. Jesus told them, "wait for the promise of the Father, which, He said, you have heard from Me." (Acts 1:4) And then when they were "with one accord" (Acts 2:1) the promise was given to them. The power of God from heaven came unto His apostles. But who is willing to believe like that? Who is willing to come together and wait for the promises of the Father to be fulfilled? We don't need more of us, we need more of Him, brothers. We don't need more religion, need more of Christ in us, the hope of glory! (Colossians 1:27)

"Be still and know that I AM God." (Psalm 46:10) "Those who wait upon the Lord . . ." (Isaiah 40:31) they will receive the reward. We come unto the fullness of Christ by the Spirit of the Living God, who is working to complete what He began in us so long ago. And He will not stop until it is done. Soon we will see more clearly. Our Father, He is God, before Him there is no other! "Hear O Israel, the LORD our God is One Lord." (Deuteronomy 6:4)

Let's come together in this Spirit of Truth, in His Holy Spirit and receive of Him, even as we wait. He will have His way in us, equip us, prepare us and send up forth; even as an army is sent out to war!

Δ   Ω

Peter, James, John, Paul, etc. those first apostles of the Lamb, they were the first brothers who learned to live as the sons of God. They received all these things from their Father and then they wrote them down for us to have in these last days. We don't have to start over from the beginning; our Father has preserved His Word for us, throughout the generations. And "the glory of the latter house will be [in fact] greater than the glory of the former." (Haggai 2:9) whose temple are we.

"Be glad then, ye children of Zion, and rejoice in the LORD your God: for He hath given you the former rain moderately, and He will cause to come down for you the rain, the former rain, and the latter rain in the first month." (Joel 2:23) In the same way that the glory of the latter house will be greater so the abundance of latter rain coming will be even greater than the former! "Greater works than these you shall do." (John 14:12) because Jesus has gone to be with the Father. And we are in Christ, Christ is in the Father and His Spirit is in us; and we are together in Him! (John 17)

Our Father celebrates in our unity. Did you know that? "Behold, how good and how pleasant it is for [the brothers] to dwell together in unity." (Psalm 133) But it is very hard to dwell in unity with this flesh. So the flesh has to go. It is very hard to be together, in love, with strife, contentions, striving, anger, malice, unforgiveness, bitterness, lust and other kinds of iniquity. Our Father wants to celebrate with us. Did you ever hear that before? He is overjoyed by our friendship, our true fellowship; Our Father delights in it. He delights in our togetherness and in our love, one for another.

This is the gospel we have received of Him. "And [then] this gospel of the kingdom will be preached in all the world as a witness to all the nations, and then the end will come." (Matthew

24:14) God is restoring to us the fullness of the gospel, Jesus never started a religion, He gave us back our Father. Now are we the sons of God. It's such an incredible story!

Let's go and tell the whole world about it!

Δ   Ω

Brothers, do you know what we will do together when His Kingdom comes? We will praise His holy name, we will worship and we will also share stories of what God did in our lives. "For the testimony of Jesus is the spirit of prophecy." (Revelation 19:10) We will sit around glorifying The Son of God as we share all that He did for us in this life. And the Lord will come and He will show us even more that we could not see. And we will glorify Him in all that He did for us.

We are His work, brothers. We are not our own works and we are not working to change our brothers, He is the Potter and we are the clay (Isaiah 64:8). We encourage the body of Christ into His presence, to trust, to surrender and we can go to Him together. But He remains God. We might be little gods (Psalm 82) but He is the Big Daddy God. Let us come to serve the Body in love, in surrender, with patience and long-suffering.

And we are in fact the Body of Christ. We are not Christ but we are His Body. Pray about this and more will be revealed. We are His Body left upon the earth, we are the light of the world and the salt of the earth (Matthew 5:13-16). The salt preserves and the light holds the darkness at bay. But what if the salt looses it savor? Or what if the light becomes dim or is put out? Even so, let us shine the Light of the Father before men.

I look forward to being with many of you. I look forward to joining with you and the other brothers. But it's much better that Christ would come to you. He is risen from the dead. Our Savior Lives. Call upon His holy name and He will come to you. Where two or three are gathered together in His name, He is there, in our midst. (Matthew 18:20)

These testimonies are exciting but it's going to get even more amazing than this before the end. There are many more things I want to discuss with you brothers, but for now this is the grace I have been given. I have been praying about what else to share, but this is the encouragement the Lord has given me to write for now.

There is new wine for us. There are also new wineskins for the new wine. Now some will say, "The old is better." But our Lord told us, "Drink the new wine." (Luke 5:36-39) Jesus' first miracle was water into wine. Then the man who was running the wedding for the groom, said, "Every man at the beginning sets out the good wine, but you have saved the best for last." (John 2:1-11) Jesus has saved the best wine for these last days. He has saved the best for us.

I love you brothers, I really do. You guys really have my heart. I have been laying down my life for Christ but now also for you guys. I really want to see us all come into this place of Great Abundance and Fullness in Christ. I really want to see Jesus' Church come into the fullness of all that He has for us. I am eager to see Him bring us there. I am very eager to see Him. I am completely convinced: it's going to get even better than this!

He is sweeping us off of our feet. We are going to get *caught up* in His goodness. We are going to get caught up in the love of God; and we won't come back down. He is doing it. We are not convincing ourselves of His love, He is opening our eyes to seeing Him like never before. He is truly turning our mourning into dancing and our weeping into rejoicing. (Jeremiah 31:10-14) In the same way God preserved His Israel in the midst of Egypt as all the plagues were raining down upon them, He will preserve us. Do not be afraid, brothers.

Be not afraid. The God we serve, He is strong and mighty. His love is powerful. He will always come through for us. We will fall, everyone of us will fall short of the glory of God but He will never fall, He will never fail us; He will always come through for us, brothers. We have nothing to fear. "God is love." (I John 4:8)

So let's go to Him. Let's sit at His feet and learn of His ways. Let's come together in true fellowship and glorify our God. Let's surrender these fallen things to Him and let Him completely have His way in us. He will show us His love. He will bring us to life and we will live it more abundantly. And He will send us out to go and tell the world, *Jesus saves*. The love of God has been revealed to us.

It's a good time to be with our Father. It's a good time to be with our brothers. It's a good time to receive the fullness Jesus has for us, by His Spirit. And then we will go and give it out to the world! And until then we can start with our neighbor. We can go and love them . . .

We receive His love so that we can go and give it. Jesus says, "My cup runneth over". It's the love of God. He was so full of God's love that whoever bumped into Him got some of it spilled out on them!

This is how they will know us, brothers
Not by our mere religion
They will know us by our love
And for those who know His name they call Him, Jesus
He is the love of God on display
Amen.